The Forbidden Fruit Or The Forbidden Truth...In The Bible?

Terry J Rowan

ISBN: 978-1-0881-2274-7

Printed in the United States of America

DEDICATION

My Mother, who pushed me to finalize this book whenever I lost

the desire to do so. Her constant soft and sobering interrogation;

while lying disabled in her bed; "Son, where you at with your

book?" Energized my spirit when the breath of motivation had left.

She left this realm in September 2021, twelve days after her

Eighty-Second birthday. I apologize for being tardy, but hopefully,

our message is on time.

When you adopt a God or Religion who is not of your own image,

When you embrace literature that teaches you to hate yourself,

and love an oppressor, When the oppressor and savior,

and your God, are one and the same,

You become the principal agent of your

mental and spiritual destruction."

Pastor, Dr. Ray Hagins

TABLE OF CONTENTS

CHAPTER ONE

THE OPENING

The Great Debate, hosted by Harold Muhammed of the Nation of Islam, Mosque #46, New Orleans, on September 8, 1991. Participants included Attorney and Reverend A. Morgan Bryant, Jr., and his opponent, Doctor Khalid Muhammad, Associate Director of the Urban Crisis Center in Atlanta, Georgia. When I attended this debate at the Mahalia Jackson Auditorium in New Orleans, I was unaware of its lengthy time span. Due to time preservation, I am giving you the reader's digest version of the event.

The Moderator takes over from here:

A discussion of the debate was originated by Carl Galmon, a local Social Activist in the New Orleans area, when he read an article printed in the local newspaper; Times Picayune, written by Reverend Bryant, in which he titled "Jesus Is Not of African Origins, Nor Is He Black." (I am very familiar with that newspaper. When I was ten years old, I had a paper route that consisted of forty customers. I delivered the States Item newspaper six days per week, then the Times Picayune paper on Sunday mornings. I understand now that both newspapers merged into the Times Picayune. I was a paper boy for three consecutive years. At age ten, I began piano lessons. And that morphed into me playing woodwind instruments.

I was also in the Boys Scout at age ten. My brother was elected Scouts Leader and Mr. Woody White was our Scouts Master. The local church I grew up in sponsored the boy's scouts for our neighborhood. I owe many expressions of gratitude to Saint John's Baptist Church, in New Orleans).

When pressed by local activists in the New Orleans area as to what was his motive in publishing such inflammatory article one week prior to Easter Sunday, when millions of Christian believers around the world begin to celebrate the crucifixion and resurrection of Jesus the Christ. Reverend Bryant did not respond to Carl Galmon letter of inquiry. So then, Carl Galmon submitted his own written article to the Times Picayune, but the newspaper refused to publish his article in their paper. They were satisfied with Reverend Bryant slanted slander only.

However, the two sides did agree to a debate to discuss the topic Reverend Bryant published.

I begin my book with excerpts of the debate titled "Jesus of the Holy Bible was a Jew, And not of Black African Origins." The narrator of the debate began with the introduction of both participants.

Attorney A Morgan Bryant was born in New Orleans, he graduated with a B.A. in Sociology, he received an M.S. in Psychology, and a Jurist Doctrine from LSU Law Center.

He served in the U.S. Air Force during 1951-1955, and has been practicing law in New Orleans since 1956.

He was a founding Senior Partner, an Arbitrator for the American Arbitration Association, and is listed in "Who's Who" in the World.

"Who's Who" 'in America, "Who's Who" in America Law, "Who's Who" in Religion, and past president of the New Orleans Baptist Theological Seminary Board of Trustee.

He was the Special Assistant Attorney General for the State of Louisiana from 1982-1987. And he is also a Lecturer.

Our Second Participant is:

Doctor Khalid Muhammed is Associate Director of the Urban Crisis Center in Atlanta Georgia, he taught in the African Studies Department at Cal State at Los Angeles, and was a recipient of the Ford Foundation.

He appeared in Public Enemy music video "Fight the Power" featuring rapper Ice-Cube and song track for Spike Lee movie "Do The Right Thing."

He is the Minister of Mosque Number Seven, in Harlem New York.

Moderators privilege provided that the Attorney Reverend Bryant begin the debate.

CHAPTER TWO

THE GREAT DEBATE

"I would know nothing among you save Jesus Christ and him crucified. I'm not a Reverend, I'm a layman. I'm a Reverend of a local Baptist Church. I'm not a ordain Minister. I am a practicing lawyer.

But I want to tell you something about where I come to this, or dialogue as I was lead to believe this is going to be. I don't pretend to try and convince you of my point of view through rhetoric, but I don't plan to use rhetoric tonight because I don't think rhetoric is what's involved in trying to present a point of view of the Lord Jesus Christ.

Secondly, I'm not here to argue the point. I'm going to present you the best I can, and as best, the Lord allows me to do so in my view of the subject.

How God works in the hearts of each of us in terms of our beliefs, or what we believe, or don't believe, what we accept, or don't accept. That's up to him and his Holy Spirit as he deals with the hearts and minds of men, and women, human beings. I don't believe in arguing points of this sort. And I will not argue them. I will try to discuss them as best I can.

I am also coming to you from the perspective of not considering this a great debate as it's been declared in these comments.

I don't know where that came off...great debate. I'm not a great debater. I'm an ordinary layman who had a point of viewpoint and I express it in a letter to the editor of the Picayune. And incidentally, the letter that appeared edited out all the scriptures I reference. Hence, those of you who read the letter in the column didn't get the benefit of the perspective that was major in my viewpoint. that were in my letter to the editor. And that it was from a biblical perspective.

I'm not competent to debate Dr Khalid on matters of the Quran. I confess to you I don't know much about the Quran. As an educated person, I know what it is, but I've never studied it, I never read it, and I don't purport to be any kind of articulator of things in the Quran.

I was simply asked over the telephone the morning after the letter appeared in the Picayune. Would you be willing to debate with somebody the point that you expressed in the letter? And I said certainly. But I am doing it from a biblical perspective.

I became a Christian forty years ago. I was in my middle year of law school at LSU. Prior to that, I had been an arrogant, cocky, smart-aleck, cynic.

I am 63 years old now. I am a deacon and a bible teacher in my church. I did not do any research in anthropology, sociology, or archaeology in ancient history probably may have a bearing on this issue. I do not have any political agendas. I am not a bigot, and I do not have any anti-black racist views despite the fact that I have a view regarding Jesus and his origins, and his ethnic background. Now after saying all of that, I will go ahead and make my presentation to you: What I believe in the bible I accepted that fact when I became a Christian that this is the inspired divinely word of

God. It is infallible. I believe it is without ERROR. Despite the fact that human beings were God instrument in writing the bible.

I don't concede that because human beings wrote the bible, it could have any errors in it. I believe that if God is overseen in his divine way, the production of what he intends to produce by these errant human being writers', God alone can control the outcome. God can see to it that the outcome is what he precisely intended. Hence, everything that the bible states to me is believable and is true. And is what God is trying to reveal through a written record, through written words to humankind. I have only two main points in my belief that Jesus was not of Black African origins. First, I believe that Jesus is plainly shown in scripture to be the divine incarnate son of God almighty Jehovah Eloheim. I believe that Jesus was God incarnate and walked upon this earth, lived on this earth for thirty-three years. I believe that the bible reveals that the line God started with Abraham and brought all the way down through the annals of time to a point where an old Jewish maiden who was chased (Mary). I don't see anything in the scriptures that teaches me that that line that I just describe is anything other than a line called Hebrew. A line called Jew, a line called Israel, a line called the seed of Abraham, a line called the Fruit of Jacob in the sense of inheritance, a line called the seed of David, a line called from the tribe of Judah of the twelve tribes that Jacob sponsor, and progenitor. I'd like to share some of those passages with you; "Now in the sixth month the angel Gabriel was sent by God to a city of Galilee named Nazareth, to a virgin named Mary saying, "Rejoice highly favored one, the Lord is with you; blessed are you among women!" (Luke 1 and 26-30)

"For you have found favor with God. And when eight days were completed for the circumcision of the Child, His name was called

Jesus, the name given by the angel before He was conceived in the womb. (Luke 2 and 21).

I am here to deal with the fact I believe strongly because the bible says so, in my opinion, that he was not from Africa. That He was from Asia Minor. And I believe He was not a Black Person, that He was a Jew. And Jews are not shown in the scriptures to be Black Persons.

The book of the genealogy of Jesus Christ, the Son of David, the Son of Abraham (Matthew 1), and Luke 3 and 25 continues with the genealogy of Jesus. The others take you to the humanity that also includes the line of the Jews. For time purposes, you can read in your own spare. So we have two genealogies, one wish takes you through the line of the Jews. The other takes you to the humanity that also includes the line of the Jews.

The Luke genealogy is broader and more extensive than the Matthew genealogy but the portion of the Luke genealogy that deals with the line from Abraham is still the Jewish line. And Jesus comes through that means. As a bible believer, I accept that. Then concerning His Son Jesus Christ our Lord who was born of the seed of David according to the flesh and declared to be the Son of God with power according to the Spirit of the dead (Romans 3 and 4). For it is evident that our Lord arose from Judah, of which tribe Moses spoke nothing concerning priesthood (Hebrew 7 and 1). So Jesus comes from the tribe of Judah, and both of the genecology's show this. And so He is a Jew from the loins of Abraham, through Isaac, through Jacob, and then through Judah one of the twelve sons of Jacob. And on down the line through the descendants of Judah of which the bible clearly demarcate. Do not weep, behold the Lion of the tribe of Judah the Root of David, has prevailed to open the scroll and to lose its seven seals.

And behold, in the midst of the throne and of the four living creatures, and in the midst of it had been slain having seven horns and seven eyes, which are the seven Sprits of God sent out into all the earth (Revelation 5 and 5-6).

If you trace through the Table of Nations in Genesis 10, I believe, and I'm not the only one to believe this. A lot of people who are in disciplines in education believe that it can be shown that the following, or some of the people, ancient people who descendent from Shem are the Jews, Arabs, Persians, and Assyrians, Babylonians are all nations who descended from Shem.

Japheth seems to have as his descendant's those who ended up occupying a part of the world Indo-China, in India, I mean Indo-Europe, India and all the northern countries in Europe, Russia, Denmark, England, Italy, Spain, France, Germany, all those Scandinavians countries. Scriptures in the Table of Nations in the tenth chapter of Genesis seems to me, to show that the descendants of Ham ended up being the following people. And there's nothing denigrating about these people. Some of these people had great civilizations, and were great nations, and had great empires. The Egyptians, Samarians, Ethiopians, Africans, Phoenicians, Mongols, Orientals, Hittites', all the Canaanites nations that ended up inhabiting the Promise Land that God had given to Abraham.

And after the exodus under Moses out of Egypt out of the Egyptians bondage where the Israelites' spent four hundred years in that bondage. They had to come back and cross over into Canaan and reestablish themselves in that promise land. Under the leadership of Joshua and Caleb they had to defeat the Canaanites'. They had to be where God intended them to be in the first place. But all of them Canaanite's nations seemingly are descendants of Ham.

I think the scriptures show that American Indians and all the South Sea Islanders are descendants of Ham. Now, what does that mean? It simply means that since Jesus descends from Shem. And not from Japeth, and not from Ham. And since the descendants of Ham seems to be the majority of people of the world who are Black in their skin pigmentation. And Black with some racial characteristics in that regard. Jesus did not descend from that line. That's why I say that Jesus is a Jew. And as a Jew, He is not a Black. And because he is from Nazareth and Bethlehem and Palestine, He is not from Africa. He is from that portion of the world that was not regarded as a part of Africa. He is from a portion of the world that is regarded as part of the continent of Asia Minor.

"I may be short of my forty-five minutes, but that is all I have to say in the opening." So, I would wager that this participant believes that the BIBLE means Basic Instructions Before Leaving Earth.

Moderator: And Now I Present to you, Minister and Doctor Khalid Muhammed:

"I am honored to debate this very important topic that Attorney Bryant has chosen the resolution to resolve that Jesus was a Jew and was not of African origin. Let's go after that...since Attorney Bryant has started off by saying ... let's look at his comments here; 'I don't plan to use rhetoric, not competent to debate on matters of the Quran,' I promise you I won't use the Quran then.

But he says he did not want to argue the point, then he should not have put it in the Times Picayune if he did not want an argument. He says tonight he wants to base much of his argument or all of his argument on the bible. On what he calls the Holy Bible.

Holy means pure book, an unmix and untampered book. And if you are going to use the Holy Bible Attorney Bryant, which Holy Bible are you going to use? Are you going to use the Scofield version? Are you going to use the Philips version? Are you going to use the Douay or Catholic version? Are you going to use the New World Translation, The Jerusalem version? What bible are you going to use is the question here tonight.

One bible has sixty-six books in it. I don't want you to miss that. Another bible has seventy-two books in it. Which bible are you going to use here tonight? We even have what's call the Forgotten Books of the bible. We've even got what's call the Lost Books of the Bible; heck who lost them?

He says that one of his contentions is that Jesus was a Jew. Well, I don't have any problem about that...lawyer. Jesus was a Jew. But now the question is, were the Jews black like me, or were the Jews white like you? Don't tell me about those over there in the illegitimate, criminal set up colony called Israel today. These are not the true Jews. These are a strain of people who have crawled out of Europe and who have driven us from power.

For years, these people have lied to us and told us that was not in Africa. Hell, you can look at it on any map. Egypt is indeed in Africa. Egypt, according to the Greeks was called the Land of the black or burnt skin people. Hieratic's, the historian wrote that the Jews of that area were dark black people. The area that is called the Middle East is really Northeast Africa separated by the mainland of Africa by a European made ditch called the Suez Canal.

All of that represented the empire of Egypt at one time. And they drove us from the sentinel of power. And all of those area's change from Black, to brown, and to white. All of the God's or Deities were depicted as Black. And as regards to Black Christ and Virgin Mary; Roman Rollin, a noted French writer says, "Why are the majority of the virgins revered, and celebrated pilgrimages Black?" He went on and talked about Zurick Switzerland, Spain, Polland. He talked to other scholars in Russia, Italy, where all of the Black Madonna, were just that. And they had a Black Baby in her arms. And you can go to this very day, all over Europe and find a Black Mary and Black Jesus.

You saw the Pope in Life Magazine bowing down and kneeling down making his prayers in front of a Black Mary and a Black Jesus, The Shrine of Czestochowa inside the Jasna Gora Monastery. Tradition says that it was St Luke who knew personally the Mother of Jesus. And he carved his hand on the majority of those black virgins, and they were spread throughout Europe. All of the God's of the known world were Black until something very significant happened.

Pope Julius commissioned a man named Michael Angelo. Michael Angelo got his uncle to pose as Adam and painted the picture. He got his aunt to pose as Eve and painted the picture. He got his cousin to pose as Jesus and painted the picture. And took the baby of his uncle and aunt to pose as the baby Jesus. Let's look at this thing a little deeper. Now the lawyer says that Jesus was a Jew and left it at that. Josephus the first century, foremost historian among the Jews; let us see what a so-called Jewish historian has to say about Jesus himself.

Now the lawyer wasn't there. I wasn't there right: But Josephus the historian of the first century A.D. had this to say: He describes Jesus as a man of simple appearance (unattractive looking), mature age, black skin, little hair, four and a half to five feet tall with a long face, and an under develop beard. He goes on to say that the early Christians, including Titulus and Saint Augustine accepted this view as the proper description of Jesus.

But now, let's go even further. In the book "Messiah Christ," by another so called Jew, since this hold thing is about Jew, that's the way you gone try and duck out of this thing, as to whether he was black or white, you gone throw a curve and try and go Jew on us. Arnold Eissler in his book "The Messiah Christ, page 411, 421, and 442, it says the paintings of Jesus after the church was allowed to come out into the open and was not banned anymore.

That the early church decided that it was offensive to the believing early Christians, and their Hellenistic idea's." So the image of Jesus having nappy hair, black skin was offensive to the church.

So, they decided to make him six feet tall, well groom, handsome, venerable, have a beautiful mouth, a full comfortable beard, and blue eyes.

The French author of his book title "The Research History of the Personality Jesus the Christ," page 2, written in 1829, says nothing remains authentic of the exterior appearance of Christ." And that the church changed all of the pictures. The bible in the book of Revelations, and the book of Daniels says that Jesus would be a man with hair like lamb's wool. His feet would be like pure brace, as if it has been burnt in an oven. So we don't argue over him being a Jew. We just know that the Jew that is over there in Israel that they call today, is not the true Jews.

That the true Hebrews is a Black Jew. It says he will have feet as though it has been burnt in an oven. Question to you audience: Does it look like Attorney Bryant has black feet to you? Does he look like he has been burnt in an over to you?

Some of the pictures of Jesus has blond hair. Some of the pictures he has red hair. Some of the pictures he has brown hair. Some of the pictures he has black hair. In other pictures, he has green eyes, hazel eyes, brown eyes, blue eyes. So I ask you audience; will the real Jesus stand up!

We don't have the Holy Bible anymore. They have changed the bible. But there is truth in the bible if we can get pass the parables, the symbols, the metaphors and the symbolism that have been added to the bible so they can deceive the very chosen people of God.

Now let's deal with this Curse of Ham that he wrote in his article about black people. He hooked us up in his article in his letter to the editor as being Ham's children and that we have been cursed. First black people, the bible does not even mention Ham being cursed. The bible says the curse was put upon Ham's unborn grandson, Canaan. The bible describes the Canaanite people as ARAB's already living in the Holy city which was ancient Palestine.

So I am not here to change this man and his nature. All of the prophets have come to them and none of them have been able to change them. So I know I can't change them.

Now I want to get back to that Revive Standard Version. Let's listen to The King James Version opening has to say…" The noblest of English prose. It expresses admiration for its simplicity, it's dignity, it's power, it's capiturn of expression.

The music of its cadences and the velocity of its rhythm. Its entrance as no other book has into the making of the personal character, as the public institution of the English-speaking people. We owe to it an incalculable debt"…I just heard that bell ring twice so my time is up."

Here, I would wager this participant believes that ISLAM means I'm Savior Lord And Master.

As to the black depictions of Jesus and Mary in Europe, I personally remember the last of my two visits to London when I patronized the downtown area one very cold Sunday evening, on my way to the West End area (The Pet Shop Boys). I saw a parade of people in the streets, bobbies, men-of-the-cloth, and women in Habits. I asked a gentleman selling newspapers behind a table, what is this? He said it is a dirge for the people who lost their lives during the explosions by the Irish Republic Army, Sein Fein. I recalled there were at least five bombs detonated that week in downtown London. Fortunate for me, I decided to stay in my room at the International Holiday-Inn on High Street Kinsington. As the marchers drew closer, I noticed one of the men in suit and tie holding a large brown wooden cross, with a statue resembling a black man, wearing a brown grass skirt, with a thorny crown on his head. I stood there statuesque for a long time. Literally! Thinking, that looks like me. When I was able to unlock my muscles, I started snapping pictures of that cross with my polaroid camera. I still have those photos to this day. In fact, I decided to use one of them for the cover of my book. I also bought a newspaper (The Sunday Times) from the new friend I met. I exhausted so much of my energy at that event, I decided to return to my hotel room for the remainder of the evening.

About the book, "Is It the Forbidden Fruit or the Forbidden Truth in the Bible," I begin with the Great Debate discussion, then I discuss the patriarch's, the patriarch's birthplace, the patriarch's ethnicity, and the patriarch's wives. From there, I focus on evidence that is recorded in many of the most respected Holy Books in the world that supports my observations. I attempt to separate the so-called myths and legions from the real and reality. I challenge the van guards who spew malicious propaganda and mischief, in the name of their beliefs, as a form of popularity or facial recognition in the religious arena. I do not imply that I uncovered every truth per se. However, I attempt to introduce to the Faithful of whatever Faith you harbor, a more critical dialogue within your arena. And also, to challenge the old generic homilies presented as the only true path to guide you through.

We all know that theology is a huge market. Many religious entities are invested in the stock market. I will not give any names, or even the ticket tape numbers assigned to them on the Stock Exchange. Simultaneous with the monetary success of theology, it has the minds, or at least the attention of endless of populations. And it does not intend to move in any direction other than in which the van guards or gatekeepers, who exist in high places, feel threaten of the grip. I ask you, the audience to envision your own experience as you read the notes. Then intensely block out what have been smelted in your consciousness. I welcome your interest in this content and your comments. Meanwhile, enjoy the journey.

CHAPTER THREE
EGYPT, THE TORAH'S MADE-UP ENEMY

The crux of the Torah stories is heavily centered around the Pharoah's and the kingdoms of Egypt. I want to talk about that ancient civilization, so this audience may become familiar with who they were. The Egyptian kingdom was a massive and very complex civilization. Their advanced knowledge in science, mathematics, military warfare, and government was the envy of their times. The Pharoah's etched their stories on the walls of the great pyramids they erected. They called it Hieroglyphic. The hieroglyphic's gave birth to many stories written in the Pentateuch. It says, "Belshazzar (son of Nebuchadnezzar) the king made a great feast for a thousand of his lords. He gave the command to bring the gold and silver vessels which his father took from the temple which had been in Jerusalem to drink from. In the same hour, the fingers of a man's hand appeared and wrote on the wall of the king's palace" (Daniel 5 and1-5).

The books in Egyptian libraries were written on papyrus. This material was created from the water plant used in sheets throughout the Mediterranean world for writing or painting. But it is native to the Nile Valley River. When their civilization fell, the books confiscated from their libraries included what's known as the Rhind Mathematic Papyrus. The correct name is the Egyptian Mathematical Papyrus, because Alexander Rhind was the name of the tomb robber who looted that area then sold his stolen prizes to various museums in Europe where they are today. Those papyrus contains the values of their currency, measurements, and equation solving methods. At the same time, the Abbott Papyrus Papers were excavated and taken to foreign museums for prophet. The Abbott Papyrus are scrolls documenting the political systems of the Egyptians during the New Kingdom time period. This was the period when the Egyptians regained their economics and military dominance again by defeating the Hyksos (Persians) military.

Then there was the Papyrus Boulaq 18. This artifact list all the ruling families. And gives hints on how the servants attended to their leaders on a day-to-day basis. These papyrus dates to the Eighteenth Dynasty of the biblical figure, King Ramesses. It says, "And Joseph situated his father and his brothers, and gave them a possession in the land of Egypt, in the best of the land, in the land of Rameses" (Genesis 47 and 11).

It says, "Then the children of Israel journeyed from Rameses to Succoth, about six hundred thousand men on foot, besides children" (Exodus 12 and 37).

Again, it says, "They departed from Rameses in the first month, the day after the Passover the children of Israel went out with boldness in the sight of all the Egyptians. For the Egyptians were burying all their firstborn, whom the Lord had killed among them. Also, on their gods the Lord had executed judgements." (Numbers 33 and 3-4). These two time periods cover the stories of both Joseph and Moses.

It is believed that the Babylonians or the Chaldeans were the originators of the zodiac. They did so by dividing the sky into twelve sections and gave meanings to each one based on the stars they align with. From there, it is suggested that an individual's destiny was determined by whatever section or sign he or she was born under. From the Babylonian kingdom, the science of astrology is believed to have been passed down to the empire of ancient Egypt. The Egyptians constructed their pyramids with certain mathematical relationships to the stars. Their sphinx has astrological significance. It has the head of a woman, symbolizing Virgo, or the virgin. And the body of a lion, symbolizing Leo. By the time the children of Israel departed Egypt, they were well versed in the science of astrology. It says, "Give no regard to spirits and wizards; do not seek after them, to be denied by them; I am the Lord your God" (Leviticus 19 and 31).Not only did astrology affect the Israelite's but the Grecians, and Romans as well. The writers of the Torah implies that astrology is a form of demonism or satanism. The writers impose their belief that it is satan that is being worshiped in the guise of the signs or the planets. They mix in the story of the Tower of Babel. But they align that story with Nimrod and his kingdom in Babylon. It is only when astrology reaches Egypt, the practice of demonism is implied.

Back to the Egypt, as the enemy point of view. The story begins with Abram, the son of Terah. It says, "This is the genealogy of Terah: Terah begot Abram (Chaldea), Nahor, and Haran (Turkey), Haran begot Lot" (Gen 11 and 27-28), whose father was Shem. The Lord found favors in Abram the Hebrew and instructed him and his wife Sarai to leave the Land of Ur in the Land of the Chaldeans. It says, "The Lord had said to Abram: Get out of your country from your family. And from your father's house. To a land that I will show you. I will make you a great nation; I will bless you and make your name great. I will bless those who bless you, and I will curse him who curses you."

So Abram departed as the Lord had spoken to him. Then Abram took Sarai his wife and Lot his brother's son, and all their possessions that they had gathered, and they departed to the Land of Canaan. And the Canaanites were then in the land" (Gen 12 and 1-6).

The story continues saying, "Now there was a famine in the land (Canaan), and Abram went down to dwell in Egypt" (Gen 12 and 10).

Prior to Abram's arrival, he was nothing but a sand desert dwelling man on a journey. But after his arrival and departure out of Egypt, Abram became a very wealthy man. The story says, "Then Abram went up from Egypt, he and his wife and all that he had, and Lot with him, to the South. Abram was very rich in livestock, in silver, and in gold. And he went on his journey from the South as far as Bethel (modern-day Jerusalem)" (Gen 13 and 1-4).

Lot, the nephew of Abram also became very wealthy during his sojourn in Egypt. The story of the Israelite's illustrates that they only became wealthy if they lived in Egypt.

So Abram, the Hebrew was to become the father of many nations. But his wife Sarai was barren. So Abram needed to find a woman; who was not his wife, and who was fertile in order for him to implement the Lord's promise. It says, "Sarai, Abram's wife, took Hagar, her bondswoman, the Egyptian, and gave her to her husband Abram to be his WIFE after Abram had dwelt in Canaan ten years. So He went into Hagar, and she conceived." (Gen 16 and 3-4)

They named the child Ishmeal. And Sarai immediately began to harbor enmity toward Hagar and her stepson. The story then informs

Hagar that his son Ishmael will grow to be a wild man, and his hand will be against every man (Gen 16 and 12-13). So Hagai, the Egyptian woman, disappear with Ishmael. And later, Ishmael became a powerful nation to this day.

Then the Lord said to Abram, you will no longer be called Abram; your name will be Abra-HAM, for I have made you a father of many nations. I will make you fruitful, I will make nations of you, and kings will come from you, I will establish my covenant between me and you and your descendants after you for the generations to come, to be your God and the God of your descendants after you. (Gen 17 and 3-7). Now acknowledge what just happened? The Lord did not consummate his covenant with Abram the Hebrew, until "Ham" was added to his name. The Lord did not add Shem or Japeth but Ham. Because HAM was added to the Lord's covenant with Abram and his seeds, the Torah scribblers will spew intense animosity towards the Hamitic people for the remainder of their existence.

Abraham had a second wife name Keturah an Ethiopian woman. It says, "Abraham again took a wife, and her name was Keturah. And she bore him Zimran, Jokshan, Madan, Midian, Ishbak, and Shuah" (Genesis 25 and 1-4).

The writers of the Abraham story chose to distance Abraham second wife, and their six sons out of the Abrahamic bloodline. They went as far as changing her wife status to that of a concubine. It says, "Now the sons born to Keturah, Abraham's concubine" (1 Chronicle 1 and 32). This was done in order to disgrace the lineage of Abraham and his seeds with Keturah. However, I conclude that 'wife' is the proper title here; in that the bible says, "If a man entice (engage in intercourse) with a virgin, who is not betroth (married or engage), and he lies with her, he shall surely pay the bride price for her to be his wife" (Exodus 22 and 16). To this day, Theologian, Historians, Lecturer's, Educators around the globe discard this fact in an all-out effort to erase at best, or mislead at worse, the true identities of Abraham seed with Hagar the Egyptian, Keturah the Ethiopian and Sarai the Chaldean.

Whether Keturah was Abraham's wife or concubine, the two of them bore Hamitic offspring as the Lord promise would occur when He added Ham to his name. It is also recognized that Sarai was barren. But she gave birth to Isaac, the last of the Abrahamic progeny.

But the question is, was Abraham the true father of Isaac? I pose this question in that, Genesis 21 and 1 says, "and the Lord visited Sarai as He said, and the Lord did for Sarai as He had promised. For Sarai conceived and bore Abraham a child in his old age." So whatever happened with Sarai and the Lord's spoken promise to her; the Hagar event is clear and explicit. It says, "So he (Abraham) went in to Hagar and she conceived" (Gen 16 and 4). It says, "Abraham took a wife name Keturah and she bore him six sons (Genesis 25 and 1). The Sarai story is not that explicit. Instead, it speaks of a promise to her made by the Lord.

According to the writers of these stories, Abraham was the Stepfather of Isaac, just like Joseph was the Stepfather of the Messiah Christ written of in the Injeel. Neither Abraham nor Joseph participated in the birth of these berths. So the Sarai and Isaac story should be identified as the first Immaculate Conception in the bible. It predates the Mary and Messiah Christ story. Or it could be said that the Mary story is merely a xerox copy of the Sarai story.

With the invention of the machine called the printing press, eventually, the writers of Sarai and Isaac fable were alerted to correct themselves in (1 Chronical 1 and 34) where they inserted "And Abraham begot Isaac."

The story goes on to say that Sarah tormented and tortured Hagar during her pregnancy with Ishmeal. She even asked Abraham to exile Hagar once Ishmeal was born. It says, "Do not let it be displeasing in your sight because of the lad or because of your bondswoman (female slave). Whatever Sarah has said to you, listen to her voice, for in Isaac your seed shall be called. Yet I will also make a nation of the son of the bondwoman, because he is your seed" (Gen 21 and 12-13). So they became a great nation living in the wilderness of Paran (Sanai). The story also talks about Egyptians being bondsmen and bondswomen to the Hebrews living in Canaan. I ask, was the enslavement of the Israelites revenge when the Lord entice them to relocate and resettle in the Land of the Egyptians?

The story says, saying that Abraham and Sarah were up in old age and was still living in the Land of Canaan. The Land allotted to Ham's children in the Table of Nations after the flood.

"There Abraham made his eldest servant swear by the Lord that he would not take a woman from the Canaanite's to marry his youngest son Isaac among whom you dwell" (Gen 24 and 3).

So the servant asked if he should take young Isaac back to the Land Abraham and Sarah came from (which was Egypt), to find a wife? But Abraham instructed his servant not to take the child back to Egypt, because the Lord told Abraham that from his descendants, they would be given this Land (Canaan), the Land flowing with milk and honey. That He will send His angel before you, and you shall take a wife for my son from their" (in Canaan after all), (Gen 24 and 5-10).

But the servant left Canaan and crossed the Mesopotamian River into the city of Nahor, or modern-day Iraq. Nahor is also called Chaldea, Babylon, and Assyria in other verses in the bible.

And there in Nahor, the servant found Rebekah to marry Isaac. Rebekah; the Chaldean woman, is described as a beautiful woman, a virgin that no man had known her (had no relations). The story says, "She gave the servant, and his camels water to drink from her pitcher of water. And for that, the servant put the ceremonious ring in her nose, and bracelets on her wrists. Then he bowed to pray to the Lord (not the angel) for leading him in the way of the truth to take the daughter of my master brother for his son (Gen 24 and 47-49).

But the Lord's instruction was for the servant to find a wife for Isaac where Abraham was living. Abraham was on his death bed living in Canaan at the time. The instructions was that Isaac should not marry a Canaanite woman.

The story goes on to say that both Abraham and Sarah died in Canaan and were buried by two of their son's; Ishmeal and Isaac who had immediately blossomed into teenage or manhood. The two buried their parents in a space called Ephron which is a burial plot near the West Bank in Jerusalem (Gen 25:9-10). So Ishmeal, the child that was exiled and left to perish in the wilderness by Sarah was laid to rest by him. The burial ceremony of Abraham and Sarah does not include Keturah and her five sons. I say five sons because the Lord killed one of them because he was wicked in his sight. This omission is purposely done in order to erase Keturah, Abraham's Ethiopian widow, from the Abrahamic blood line.

Rebekah and Isaac married each other, but Rebekah was barren, just like her deceased mother-in-law Sarah. So Isaac prostrated to the Lord for Rebekah to conceive his children, and the Lord heard his prayers. Rebekah was impregnated with twin boys.

It says, "The twins struggle inside of her, so Rebekah went into prayer and the Lord said to her, "Two nations are in your womb, two people shall be separated from your body; One shall be stronger than the other, and the Older shall serve the younger" (Gen 25 and 23). The first born of the twins came out red and hairy like a hairy garment all over. And he was named Esau, who grew up and became a great hunter.

The story continues saying that the second twin came out with his hand grabbing hold of Esau heels. And he was named Jacob. The crux of this story is to relay that the twins represented two different nations that were physically fighting inside the womb of Rebekah. The story says, "Now it came to pass, when Isaac was old and his eyes were so dim that he could not see, that he called Esau his older son (Esau) and said to him. My son I do not know the day of my death. Take your weapons, your quiver and your bow, and go out to the field and hunt game for me.

And make me savory food, such as I love, and bring it to me that I may eat, that my soul may bless you before I die. Rebekah, his wife was listening when Isaac spoke to Esau his son. She spoke to Jacob her son; and said; go now to the flock and bring me from there two choice kids of the goats, and I will make savory food from them for your father, such as he loves. Then you shall take it to your father, that he may eat it, and that he bless you before his death.

And Jacob said to Rebekah, look, Esau my brother is a hairy man, and I am a smooth skinned man. Perhaps my father will feel me, and I shall seem to be a deceiver to him, and I shall bring a curse on myself and not a blessing. But his Mother said to him, let your curse be on me, my son. Only obey my voice and go. Afterwards,

Rebekah made savory food, then Rebekah took the choice clothes of her elder son Esau, which were with her in the house, and put them on Jacob. And she put the skins of the kids of the goats on his hands and on the smooth part of his neck. Jacob said to his father, I am Esau your firstborn, I have done just as you told me. Please arise, sit and eat of my game, that your soul may bless me. But Isaac said, how is it that you have found it so quickly my son? And he said, Because the Lord your God brought it to me (his Mother, Rebekah he was describing as Lord God). Then Isaac said to Jacob, come near, that I may feel my son whether you are really my son Esau or not. So Jacob went near and he felt him and said, the voice is Jacob's voice, but the hands are the hands of Esau. He did not recognize him because his hands were hairy like his brother Esau's hand, so he (Isaac) blessed him (Jacob).

And he said and kiss me, and he came near and kissed him, and he smelled the smell of his clothing, and blessed him and saying Let peoples serve you and nations bow down to you. Be master over your brethren and let your Mother's sons bow down to you. Cursed be everyone who curses you. And blessed be those who bless you! (Gen 27 and 1 thru 29).

According to Isaac, this was supposed to be the blessings passed down to Esau, not Jacob. Isaac knew that his older son Esau was not present in the room the time he took his last breath. He also knew that his wife Rebekah colluded with Jacob to deceive him. If Isaac didn't know, then certainly the Lord God knew. Because it was the Lord who orchestrated the entire deception. How is it that a Lord God be a party to a thief then try to disguise it? The Holy Quran says, "And not the weight of an atom in the earth or in the heaven is hidden from thy Lord" (Sura 10 and 61, Jonah).

Moving on, it says that Esau plotted to murder his brother Jacob for this deceit and his theft. But he then found love, and eventually married a Egyptian woman named Mahalath, who was the daughter of Ishmeal. (Gen 28 and 9). Jacob traveled eastward to a city name Haran; (Turkey today), and met Rachel, the Armenian daughter of Nahor. The author confuses the reader in two parts here. In Genasis 29 and 4-6 it says, "And Jacob said to them, My brethren, where are you from? And they said, we are from Haran. Then he said to them, do you know Laban the son of Nahor? And they said, we know him. So he (Jacob) said to them, is he well? And they said, he is well. And look, his daughter Rachel is coming with the sheep. That verse put Rachel in Turkey. The author writes; "Rachel came with her father's sheep, for she was a shepherdess. And it came to pass, when Jacob saw Rachel the daughter of Laban his mother's brother, he kissed her, and lifted up his voice and wept." The question to ask, is Nahor the father of Rachel, or is Laban the father of Rachel?

After closer research, Jacob is a distant relative of Rachel, in that Jacob's Mother Rebekah was the sister of Laban. And Laban is the son of Nahor, who was the father of both Rebekah and Laban. So then, Rachel is the daughter of Laban. And Jacob fell in awe with her upon first site. Then the two first cousins began an incestuous matrimony. We are discovering that the book is not fallible as Attorney Reverend Bryant proclaim in his opening. The story says, "Jacob agreed to work seven years for Laban in order to marry his daughter Rachel.

However, since Rachel was the youngest daughter, Laban brought Leah, his oldest daughter for Jacob after his seven years was fulfilled. Because it was not customary for the younger to be given into marriage before the eldest daughter. So Jacob agreed to work another seven years for Laban in order to wed Rachel. After the second seven years, Rachel was given to Jacob to wed (Gen 29 and

16-30). Laban gave to Jacob as a bonus for his diligence to wed Rachel, two of his slave women named Zilpah to serve Leah. And Bilhah to serve Rachel.

Rachel, the Armenian was barren and could not have children. Just like Sarah, and Rebekah before her. So Jacob, and Leah, and the two bondswomen, Zilpah and Bilhah began having relations, and they begat the so-called "selected" children of Israel. I say selected because the children of Hagai, Keturah, and Zipporah were not selected in these narratives. The story says in (Genasis 30 and 1 thru 21):

Reuban-was Leah's first child	Simeon- was Leah's second child	Levi-was Leah's third child
Judah-was Leah's fourth child	Issachar- was Leah's fifth child	Zebulun-was Leah's sixth child
Dina was Leah's seventh child	Dan was Bilhah first child	Naphtali-was Bilhah second
Gad-was Zilpah first child	Asher-was Zilpah second child	Joseph-was Rachel first child

Then God remembered Rachel and God listened to her and opened her womb. And she conceived and bore a son, and said, God has taken away my reproach. So, she called his name Joseph and said, the Lord shall add to me another son" (Gen 30 and 22-24). The question I ask, is there a thirteenth tribe of Israel? I say No. Because Leah seventh child was a baby girl named Dinah. Her bloodline would have ended when she married. So, another male child must be born.

Jacob and his clan left Haran (Turkey) to return to Canaan (Palestine). But prior to their departure, they stole property from Laban, the uncle of Jacob, and the father of Rachel, his wife. The story says, "Now Jacob heard the words of Laban's sons, saying Jacob has taken away all that was our father's, he had acquired all this wealth. And Jacob saw the favors of Laban, and indeed it was not favorable toward him as before. Then the Lord said to Jacob, return to the Land of your fathers (Canaan) and your family and I will be with you. So Jacob sent and called Rachel and Leah to the field, to his flock and said your father has deceived me and changed my wages ten times, but God did not allow him to hurt me. So God has taken away the livestock of your father and given them to me. Then Rachel and Leah said to him, Is there still any portion or inheritance for us in our father's house?

Are we not considered strangers by him? For he has sold us and completely consumed our money. For all these riches God has taken away from our father are really ours and our children's. Then Jacob rose and set his sons and his wives on camels. And he carried away all his livestock and all his possessions which he had gained (by deceit) in Paran Aram to go to his father Isaac in the Land of Canaan. Now Laban had gone to shear his sheep, and Rachel (his daughter,) stole the household idols that were her father's. And Jacob stole away, unknown to Laban.

Here, Jacob is placed in Syria, but earlier, he was in Haran, or Turkey where he first met Laban and his wives and his concubines. So he fled with all that he had, He arose and crossed the river, and headed toward the mountains of Gilead" (Gen 31 and 1-21).

I believe the writers intentionally do not want the children of Jacob to be associated with Turkey, the place of their birth. Because Turkey is where the Ashkenazi gentiles are placed in the Table of Nations. So they selected Syria, and Persia instead. Here is an article exposing one particular DNA tracing company. The article is titled "Why Did 23andMe Tell Ashkenazi Jews They Could Be

Descended from Khazars? It says, "a large portion of Jews may be descended from the Khazars, a semi-nomadic tribe in the Caucasus that was largely destroyed in the 10th century C.E., and not from the Israelites of the Israel/Palestine area from several thousand years ago. This theory, known as the 'khazar theory'. The genomics company 23andMe has retracted a statement made on the profiles of Ashkenazi heritage."

Whenever the truth be told, discreditation and backlash appears. My observation is creditable in that the writer's already whited out Hagar the Egyptian, and her son Ishmeal, Abram's first-born child. The writers also eliminated the six sons of Keturah, the Ethiopian wife of Abraham the Covenant bearer, completely out of the Abrahamic bloodline. However, The Holy Quran says, "And not the weight of an atom in the earth or in the heaven is hidden from thy Lord" (Sura 10 and 61, Jonah).

The story continues saying; Laban and his forces caught up with Jacob in the mountains of Gilead. And Laban asked Jacob, "Why did you flee away so secretly and steal from me, and not tell me." And Jacob replied, "Because I was afraid. Perhaps you would take your daughters from me by force. Jacob convinces Laban to make a covenant with him and they called it Mizpah, meaning God is witness between you and me" (Gen 31 and 25-50).

"Dinah, the only daughter of Jacob, was raped and violated by Shechem, who was a prince in Caanan. And after the assault, Shechem asked his father Hamor to negotiate with Jacob to give his daughter to him in marriage (which was customary to do if the woman was not married or betroth). Jacob and his son's first refused the plea saying we cannot do this thing to give our sister to one who is uncircumcised, for that would be a reproach to us. But on this condition, we would consent if every male of you is circumcised, then we will give our daughter to you, and we will take your daughters to us and we will become one people. So, Prince Shechem agreed, and immediately spoke to all the men in their city saying, these men are at peace with us. So he thought.

Therefore, let them dwell in the Land and trade. For indeed, the Land is large enough for them. Now on the third day of circumcision, every male in the city was still in pain. Simeon and Levi took swords and killed all the males. Then they went across the city of Caanan and plundered. Then they went to the prince house and killed both Shechem and his father Hamor with the edges of the sword, and took Dinah from Shechem's house, and went out. The sons of Jacob came upon the slain and plundered the city because their sister had been defiled. They took their sheep, their oxen, and their donkeys, what was in the city and what was in the field, and all their wealth. All their little ones and their wives they took captive, and they plundered even all that was in the houses" (Gen 34 and 14-29).

To believe that only two men, with two swords, successfully slain an entire city of teenage boys, and men, by themselves is to believe that your brain is still normal after having a lobotomy.

CHAPTER FOUR

JACOB BECOMES ISRAEL AND A SON IS BORN

"Then God said to Jacob, Arise, go up to Bethel (a city in Canaan), and dwell there, and make an altar there to God, who appeared to you when you fled from the face of Esau your brother. Then God appeared to Jacob again, when he came from Padan Aram (Syria) and blessed him. And God said to him; Your name is Jacob, your name shall not be called Jacob anymore, but "Israel" shall be your name. So, He called his name Israel. Also, God said to him; I am God Almighty, Be fruitful and multiply; a nation and a company of nations shall proceed from you, and kings shall come from you, and your body.

The land which I gave Abraham and Isaac, I give to you, and to your descendants after you I give this land. Then God went up from him in the place where He talked with him. So Jacob set up a pillar in the place where He talked with him, a pillar of stone; and he poured a drink offering on it, and he poured oil on the place where God spoke with him and called it Bethel" (Gen 35 and 1-15). It should be added here that the Lord never gave the land of Canaan to Abraham or Isaac. Instead, the Lord made a promise to give Canaan to their descendants. Multiple misconceptions are found in this single passage.

The story begins with God commanding Jacob to go to Bethel, then concludes with; Jacob calling the Holy Site where he spoke with God, Bethel, the same name. Also, I observed that there was a scramble to erase the stench associated with the name Jacob; so God (i.e., the storytellers) change's his name to "Israel."

After all the hullabaloo, the storytellers introduce the missing boy child needed to replace Dinah, the girl child of Leah. It says, "Then they journeyed from Bethel. Rachel labored in childbirth, and she had hard labor. Now it came to pass when the midwife said to her, 'Do not fear you will have this son.' And it was as her soul was departing, for she had died, and his father called him Benjamin. So, Rachel died and was buried on the way to Bethlehem. And Jacob set a pillar of her grave, which is the pillar of Rachel's grave to this day (Gen 35 and 19-20). The story then concludes with adding Benjamin to the clan. It says, "These were the sons of Jacob who were born to him in Padan Aram," which is Syria today (Gen 35 and 26). May we recall earlier the author put the birth of the twelve tribes in Syria when most were born in Paran, or Turkey. The deceptions even fooled the author, it appears.

We latter see that Isaac was of old age and he perished. The story says, "Then Jacob came to his father Isaac in Hebron, where Abraham and Isaac had dwelt. So Isaac breath his last and died, and was gathered to his people. And his sons Esau and Jacob buried him (Gen 35 and 27-29). "Now Jacob dwelt in the land where his father (Isaac) was a stranger, in the land of Canaan. This the history of Jacob" (Gen 37 and 1). Isaac and his parents were not strangers in Canaan. They lived, died, then buried in Canaan.

"Joseph was feeding the flock with his brothers. And the lad was with the sons of Bilhah and Zilpah, his father's wives (here, Bilhah and Zilpah were wives of Jacob, and not his concubines), and Joseph brought a bad report of them to his father. Israel (Jacob) loved Joseph more than all his children, because he was the son of his old age" (Gen 37 and 1-3). Joseph was the first born of Rachel. Then her birth to Benjamin, made him the youngest child of the thirteen. It is unclear why Joseph became the most loved.

But I digress and continue with the storyline, with his brothers plot to murder him because of their enmity towards him. It says, "His brothers said to him, Shall you indeed reign over us? Or shall you indeed have dominion over us? So they hated him even more (Gen 37 and 8). But it was Reuben, the son of Leah that thwarted the murder plot. It says, "Reuben heard it, and he delivered him out of their hands, and said, let us not kill him. Shed no blood but cast him into this pit with no water in it, which is in the wilderness. Then they lifted their eyes and there was a company of Ishmaelites (Egyptians), coming from Gilead (Canaan) with their camels returning to Egypt. So Judah (Leah's fourth son) said to his brothers, what profit is there if we kill our brother and conceal his blood?

Let us sell him to the Ishmaelites and let not our hand be upon him. Then the Midianites (Ethiopians, previously the writer wrote Ishmaelites) traders passed by, the brothers sold him to the Ishmaelites for twenty shekels of silver. And they took Joseph to Egypt (Gen 37 and 21-28). So Joseph was placed in prison in Egypt by Potiphar, a captain in Pharoah's guard unit, for erroneously trying to assault his wife. The story says, "Joseph was handsome in form and appearance, his master's (Potiphar) wife cast longing eyes on Joseph, and she said Lie with me.

41

But he refused and said How then can I do this great wickedness, and sin against God? So it was, as she spoke to Jospeh day by day, that he did not heed her. Joseph went into the house to do work, and none of the men was inside, that she caught him by his garment, saying Lie with me. But he left his garment in her hand and fled. When she saw he left his garment in her hand, she called to the men and spoke to them, saying, See, he has brought in to us a Hebrew to mock us. He came in to me to lie with me and I cried out with a loud voice. So she kept his garment until his master came home" (Gen 39 and 6-16). While incarcerated, Joseph was given favor by the prison guards. The story says, "The keeper of the prison committed to Joseph's hand all the prisoners who were in the prison" (Gen 39 and 22). The keeper of the prison did not look into anything that was under Joseph's authority" (Gen 39 and 23). Then Pharoah had a dream, better describe as a nightmare. A dream that he called his magicians and wise men to interpret for him, but they could not. One of Pharoah's butlers informed him of Joseph, and the nightmare he interpreted for him while he was incarcerated. The story says, "There was a young Hebrew man with us. He interpreted our dreams for us (Gen 41 and 12). Then Pharoah summoned Joseph to unlock the mysteries of his nightmare. It says, "Then Joseph said to Pharoah, the dreams of Pharaoh are one; God has shown Pharoah what He is about to do: Indeed, seven years of great plenty will come throughout all the land of Egypt; but after them seven years of famine, and all the plenty will deplete the land Egypt" (Gen 41 and 25-30). Here, Joseph, introduces an alien authority to the Egyptian Pharoah. A name he called GOD!

I want to insert here that the Egyptians practice and worship their own ana-mystical spiritualities. And did so ages before this Hebrew man; who was once thrown into a waterless pit by his brothers, then sold for thirty shekels to Ethiopian desert merchants, ever arrived. For example, here are a few of them: Isis-The moon... Ra- the Sun (not Son) ...El-Saturn. Or better put, ISRAEL.

I also begin to question the writer's usage of the words God, and Lord. These titles do not always represent a Deity or Devine Authority. Even when the first letter is capitalized. Instead, within context, these titles are mere personifications of Rulers, Kings, and/or fierce empires of the time.

You will not find Race as we know it today, in the texts. Instead, they speak of nation and nationalities. For instance, when a writer speaks of the Egyptians, the writer does not identify them as Africans; which is not a country, but a continent with more than fifty countries within its borders. Some bible writers describe Egypt as "Goshen." It says, "Then Pharaoh spoke to Joseph, saying, your father and your brothers have come to you. The land of Egypt is before you. Have your father and brothers' dwell in the best of the land; let them dwell in the land of Goshen" (Gen 47 and 5-6 in this passage). Pharoah welcome's the arrival of Joseph family with a warm heart.

I want to interject here that this civilization identified themselves as Kemet. It is the Grecian language that dominated literature at that time period that mis-identified them as Egyptians. When an artifact was excavated from the region of Kemet, it obviously would have been written in the Kematic language. But we are led to believe that the artifacts were written in Greek etymology. So it is my belief that these stories are a postscript of ancient Egypt after it finally fell to "Alexander The Greek" military stance against Kemit. It is a documented fact that Greeks were welcome into the schools of the Egyptians to study for centuries. Greeks became full citizens in Egypt and thrived in knowledge and wealth. They were never enslaved, neither were they persecuted. They were accepted by the Kematic people, and they prospered alongside the Kematic people, just as the so-called Hebrews in these biblical writings. With great appreciation, the writer's most often provide us with geographical locations of where these empires once existed. Giving us rivers, seas, deserts, and mountains as markers of their existence.

This is what Dr Khalid alluded to in his opening, when he said, "The bible is a great tool once you begin to decipher the symbolism and artistry of its prose." He is speaking of shuffling through the word-salad used to redirect our subconsciousness away from reality. In this book, my intention is to take away the mysteries, the illusions, and to unravel the tongue twisters, that are set in place to tinker with the inner emotions, and thereby cause us to surrender logic and reason as we mature. In other words, to halt you from meta-morphing into another Attorney-Reverend Bryant, who boast about believing these are "the divine words of God." The story continues saying, that after hearing his beloved son, Joseph was alive, and living in Egypt, Jacob (now Israel) decided to go and see him. It says, "Then Israel said, it is enough. Joseph my son is still alive. I will go and see him before I die," (Gen 45 and 28). So Israel took his journey with all that he had, and came to Beersheba (the Negev desert) and offered sacrifices to the God of his father Isaac. Then God spoke to Israel in visions and said, Jacob, Jacob, here I am.

I am God, the God of your father; do not fear to go down to Egypt, I will make of you a great nation there. I will go with you to Egypt, and I will also bring you up again; and Joseph will put his hand on your eyes. Then Jacob arose from Beersheba; and the sons of Israel carried their father Jacob, their little ones, and their wives, carts which Pharaoh sent to carry him. So they took their livestock and their goods, which they had acquired in Canaan, and went to Egypt. Jacob and all his descendants with him" (Gen 46 and 1-7).

Joseph amassed an abundance of wealth and authority, after his release from prison. The story says, "Now Joseph was governor over the land; and it was he who sold to all the people of the land" (Gen 42 and 6). Joseph became so wealthy in Egypt, "That he was called the lord of the land" (Gen 42 and 30). Now his father Israel, and all his descendants were commanded to join Joseph in Egypt, bringing all the wealth they pilfered from Haran, and Canaan, while camping in their land as aliens. So, the heist of Goshen is now set in place. The empire of Kemet is the next kingdom to be overthrown. But this time, with the aide and protection of a mysterious "GOD" of Abraham, Isaac, and Jacob. It is this God terminology that I focus on from this point forward.

Continuing, Canaan always prospered when Egypt prospered. They traded relentlessly with the Egyptians for their sustenance. For example, it says, "When Jacob saw that there was grain in Egypt, Jacob said to his sons, why do you look at one another. Indeed I have heard that there is grain in Egypt; go down to that place and buy for us there, that we may live and not die" (Gen 42 and 1-2). It says, "Now there was no bread in all the land (Egypt); for the famine was very severe, so that the land of Egypt and the land of Canaan languished because of the famine. And Joseph gathered up all the money that was found in the land of Egypt and in the land of Canaan, for the grain which they bought; and Joseph brought the money into Pharaoh's house. So when the money failed in Egypt and in the land of Canaan, all the Egyptians came to Joseph and said, give us bread, for why should we die in your presence?" (Gen 47 and 13-15).

The storytellers expose they suffer from uncontrollable delusion. But their psychosis gets better. It says, "Then Joseph said, give your livestock, and I will give you bread, if the money is gone. So they brought their livestock to Joseph, and Joseph gave them bread in exchange for the horses, the flocks, the cattle of the herds, and for the donkeys. Thus, he fed them with bread in exchange for all their livestock that year" (Gen 47 and 16-18). "Then Joseph bought all the land of Egypt for Pharaoh: for every man of the Egyptians sold his field because the famine was severe upon them, but the priest did not sell their land. So the land became Pharaoh's" (Gen 47 and 20-22).

The question to ask is; If currency, bread, the livestock, and its military were still plentiful during the famine in Egypt, then what was the significance of a famine?

Joseph dwelt in the land of Egypt and his possessions there grew and multiplied exceedingly, the story says. But let us take a pause here. It would have been literally impossible for this increase in wealth, land purchasing, and multiplying birth rate to occur with only sixty-six vagabonds. It says, "All the persons who went with Jacob to Egypt, who came from his body, besides Jacob's sons, wives, were sixty-six persons in all (Genesis 46 and 26) within a seventeen year time span? It says, "And Jacob lived in the land of Egypt seventeen years" (Genesis 47 and 28). Here, you see these biblical fables are the prescription for a larger scale of corruption, territorial wars, and even international wars with only two agendas. First one is, the insatiable appetite to grab land and its material away from the indigenous peoples. And secondly, to chain the minds and to control the behaviors of individuals within cultures to believe that having pride in their contribution to the betterment of humankind is a selfish idea.

The conclusion of the Genesis narrative ends with Jacob now Israel; as they are both used interchangeable throughout the five books, dying of old age. It says, "When the time drew near that Israel must die, he called his son Joseph and said to him, now if I have found favor in your sight, please put your hand under my thigh, and

46

deal kindly and truly with me. Please do not bury me in Egypt, but let me lie with my fathers, you shall carry me out of Egypt and bury me in their burial place (Genesis 47 and 28-30). Now it came to pass after these things that Joseph was told indeed your father is sick, and he took with him his two sons, Manasseh and Ephraim. And Jacob was told, look, your son Joseph is coming to you, and Israel strengthened himself and sat up on the bed.

Then Jacob said to Joseph: God almighty appeared to me at Luz (the city of Bethel) in the land of Canaan and blessed me and said, Behold, I will make you fruitful and multiply you, and I will make of you a multitude of people, and give this land (Canaan) to your descendants after you as an everlasting possession. And now your two son Ephraim and Manasseh, who were born to you in the land of Egypt before I came to you in Egypt are mine, they shall be mines. Your offspring whom you beget after them shall be yours, they will be called by the name of their brothers in their inheritance. But as for me; when I came from Padan (Syria), Rachel died beside me in that land of Canaan, and I buried her there in Bethlehem (I believe the correct spelling is BethleHam).

Then Israel eventually blessed Joseph's two sons beginning with Ephraim, the youngest, and then Manasseh. Then Israel said to Joseph, Behold, I am dying, but God will be with you and bring you back to the land of your fathers. I have given to you one portion above your brothers, which I took from the hand of the Amorite with my sword and my bow" (Genesis 48 and 1-22).

This passage introduces the two sons of Joseph name Ephraim and Manasseh. But this passage does not give the name of the two son's mother. In a previous verse it says, "And Pharaoh called Joseph's name Zaphnath Paaneah. And he gave him as a wife Asenath, the daughter of PotiPherah, a priest" (Genesis 41 and 45).

47

So the mother of Joseph son's was another Egyptian woman named Asenath.

Continuing, Israel then gathered his sons and told them these things; "Bury me with my fathers in the cave that is in the field of Ephron the Hittite, in the cave that is in the field of Machpelah, which is before Mamre in the land of Canaan which Abraham brought with the field of Ephron as a possession for a burial place. There they buried Abraham and Sarah his wife, there they buried Isaac and Rebekah his wife, and there I buried Leah (one of Jacob's wife). And when Jacob had finished commanding his sons, he drew his feet up into the bed and breathed his last" Genesis 49 and 29-33).

The story continues, "And Joseph commanded his servants the physicians to embalm his father. So the physicians embalmed Israel. Forty days were required for him, for such are the days required for those who are embalmed; and the Egyptians mourned for him seventy. Joseph spoke to the household of Pharoah saying please let me go up and bury my father, and I will come back. And Pharaoh said, go up and bury your father, as he made you swear. So Joseph went up to bury his father, and with him went up all the servants of Pharaoh, the elders of the house, and all the elders of the land of Egypt, as well as all the house of Joseph.

Only their little ones, their flocks, and their herds they left in the land of Goshen. And there went up with him both chariots and horsemen, and it was a very great gathering." (Genesis 50 and 2-9).

So here, the writers describe how the Pharaoh granted all of Joseph requests to bury his father in the land of Canaan, the territory Egypt He defended. The story even says that Pharaoh provided an escort for Israel's burial possession to Canaan. The people in Jordan and Canaan took Joseph's family and the Egyptian montage to be one and the same people. It says, "Then they came to the threshing floor of Atad, which is beyond the Jordan, and they mourn there with a great and very solemn lamentation.

And when the inhabitants of the land, the Canaanites saw the mourning at the threshing floor, they said, "This is a deep mourning of the Egyptian's.

And after he had buried his father (Israel), Joseph returned to Egypt, he and his brothers and all who went up with him to bury his father" (Genesis 50 and 10-14).

This portion highlights that the Egyptian people and the seed of Israel were incomparable. The Canaanites and the Hittites, who were still dwelling in the land of their birth, could not tell any difference between them. No one knew more about the Egyptians than the inhabitants of Canaan. The Genesis story concludes saying, "Joseph dwelt in Egypt, he and his father's household. And Joseph lived on hundred and ten years. Joseph saw Ephraim's children to the third generation. And Joseph said to his brethren, I am dying, but God will surely visit you, and bring you out of this land to the land of which He swore to Abraham, to Isaac, and to Jacob. Then Joseph took an oath from the children of Israel saying you should carry up my bones from here. So Joseph died, being one hundred and ten years old, and they embalmed him, and he was put in a coffin in Egypt" (Genesis 50 and 22-26). Joseph requested on his dying bed that his brothers take his bones out of Egypt, but they did not. So Joseph died, and was buried in Egypt. The land where he and his family prospered. And not in Canaan where his father and mother were buried.

There are two questions I ask, as the Book of Genesis closes? First, an unknown "God" was introduced to the Pharaoh, and done so without any discussion of whom this God was/is; what direction it would come from, who is sending it, or what it's motive would serve. And last, the book provides detail descriptions of the mixture of people occupying Canaan.

It describes Syrians, Hittites and Palestinian's (Arabs), Ethiopians (Sudanese today), Egyptians, and Turkish (those currently occupying Egypt today). The question is, where are the signs of a Slavic presence in the Egypt Palestine vicinity up to this point?

After the deaths of Israel and Joseph, the story says, "And a man of the house of Levi went and took as wife a daughter of Levi. So the woman conceived and bore a son. Then she saw that he was a beautiful child, she hid him three months. But when she could no longer hide him, she took an ark of bulrushes daubed with asphalt, put the child in it, and laid it in the reeds (grass) by the river's (Nile River) bank" (Exodus 2 and 1-3). The parent of this child is not mentioned in this verse. But they are in another. It says, "Amram took for himself Jochebed, his father's sister (the nephew marries the aunt), as wife, and she bore him Aaron and Moses" (Exodus 6 and 20). Then the daughter of Pharaoh came down to bathe at the river.

And when she saw the ark among the reeds, she sent her maid to get it. And when she opened it, she saw the child, and the baby wept. So she had compassion on him, and said, this is one of the Hebrews children. Then his sister (Miriam) said to Pharaoh's daughter, Shall I go and call a nurse that she may nurse the child for you? And Pharaoh's daughter said to her, GO. Was the maiden mentioned here, Miriam, the sister of Moses?

So the maiden went and called the child's mother (Jochebed). Then Pharaoh's daughter said to her (Jochebed), Take this child away and nurse him for me, and I will give you your wages. So the woman (Jochebed) took the child and nursed him. And the child (Moses) grew, and she (Jochebed) brought him to Pharaoh's daughter, and he became her son. So she called his name Moses saying, Because I drew him out of the water" (Exodus 2 and 5-10).

The question I ask is what is the name of Pharoah's daughter? You will not find any descriptions of her in your holy books because she is intentionally whited out of their narrative. However, the Jewish Encyclopedia says this of her "God said to her, Bithiah, you have called Moses your son, therefore I will call you my daughter, (bat= daughter, and yah=God). The suffix "Yah" is not a Jewish sound. Instead, it is a Hebraic/Aramaic sound. That is why the majority of the prophets in the Old Testament name ends with the Yah sound. For example, Isaiah, Jeremiah, Joshua, Micah, Nehemiah, Obadiah, Zechariah. The spelling of these names was also changed to represent the English pronunciations and not those from their original tongue.

When Moses had matured, he went strolling the terrain and came across an Egyptian man beating a Hebrew, one of his brethren. When Moses saw the close was clear, he killed the Egyptian. The story says, "When Pharaoh heard of this matter, he sought to kill Moses. But Moses fled from the face of Pharaoh and dwelt in the land of Midian" (Exodus 2 and 15), the land of the Ethiopians. The Ethiopian people also spoke of Moses as being an Egyptian. The story says, "Now the priest of Midian had seven daughters. And they came and drew water. Then the shepherds came and drove them away, but Moses stood up and helped them and watered their flock. When they came to Reuel (Midia or Jethro) their father, he said, how is it that you have come so soon today? And they said, an Egyptian delivered us from the hand of the shepherds" (Exodus 2 and 16-19).

Moses was introduced to Ruel and was given one of his daughters to be his wife. Her name was Zipporah. What the Exodus storytellers does not mention is who the Medianite people were. However, the Prophet Amos does. The Lord said to Amos, "Are you not like the people of Ethiopia to Me (some translation says Cushite) O children of Israel says the Lord. Did I not bring up Israel from the land of Egypt" (Amos 9 and 7)? Moses and Zipporah gave birth to a son whom Moses called Gershom, meaning "I have been a stranger in a foreign land" (Exodus 2 and 21-22).

So, we have Moses the Hebrew baby, who was mistaken by the Egyptians as being one of their own growing up in the Palace, who is now married to an Ethiopian woman name Zipporah, then fathering a son name Gershom. But the Attorney Reverend Bryant teaches his bible students that Jesus was a Jew, and that Jews have no African bloodline. Well, Reverend Bryant, show your students how the storytellers have strategically erased them out of the Jew and Jesus narratives. For starters, you may require them to study my book!

CHAPTER FIVE
RITUAL'S AND SACRIFICE IN RELIGION ARE SINFUL?

When we read the practice's practice by the followers of religious beliefs in their genesis, we see actions that today would cause us to lose our liberty in a free society. Christopher Hitchens was a vocal disbeliever in the God Lord theory. He was an author from Britain, with publications catalogued in the Library of Congress, has this to say about religion and its rituals, "There are, indeed, several ways in which religion is not just amoral, but positively immoral. And these faults and crimes are not to be found in the behavior of its adherents but in its original precepts. These include:

*Presenting a false picture of the world to the innocent

* The doctrine of blood sacrifice

* The doctrine of atonement

* The doctrine of eternal reward and/or punishment

* The imposition of impossible tasks and rules

All the creation myths of all peoples have long been known to be false." He highlights the practice of blood sacrifices. For example, he writes, "Before monotheism arose, the altars of primitive society reeked of blood, much of it human and some of it infant. Pious Jews are at this moment trying to breed the spotlessly pure 'red heifer 'which if slaughtered again, will hasten the end of time and the coming of the Messiah."

Christopher is referring to the story told in the book of Numbers that says, "Now the Lord spoke to Moses and Aaron, saying, this is the ordinance of the law which the Lord has commanded, saying: Speak to the children of Israel, that they bring you a red heifer (cow) without blemish. You shall give it to Eleazar (Aaron son) the priest, that he may take it outside the camp, and it shall be slaughtered before him; and the priest shall take some of its blood with his finger, and sprinkle some of its blood seven times directly in front of the tabernacle of meeting, it is for purifying from sin. It shall be a statute forever to the children of Israel and to the stranger who dwells among them" (Numbers 19 and 1-10). The blood sacrifice of animals was mostly practiced over those of human babies.

But here was a ritual that involved the setting on fire of widows. That practice was called "SATI." Richa Jain wrote in her article that "Sati was the name of the wife of Lord Shiva. Her father never respected Shiva and often despised him. To protest against the hatred that her father held for her husband, she burned herself. While she was burning, she prayed to be reborn as Shiva's wife again. This did happen, and her new incarnation was called Parvati." She said it became a voluntary act considered courageous and heroic, for widows to set themselves of fire, but then it turned into a forced practice. She writes, "With time, it became a forced practice. Women who did not wish to die like this were forced to do so in different ways.

Traditionally, a widow had no role to play in society and was considered a burden. So, if a woman had no surviving children who could support her, she was pressurized to accept sati. Some women would jump or walk into the pyre (fire) after it had been lit, while other women would sit on the pyre and then light it themselves." Sati has been banned in India, and everywhere else, it was introduced, lets prey!

Child sacrifice, Self-mutilation was a practice in other faiths. For example,

"They filled this place with the blood of the innocents, they have also built the high places of Baal, to burn their sons with fire for burnt offerings to Baal" (Jeremiah 19 and 4-5).

"Happy is the one who seizes your infants, and gashes them up against the rocks" (Psalms 137 and 9).

"The Lord spoke to Moses, say to Aaron, take your rod and stretch out your hand over the waters of Egypt, over their streams, over their rivers, over their ponds, and over all their pools of water, that they may become blood. And there shall be blood throughout all the land of Egypt" (Exodus 7 and 19).

"When Sauls servant had told them what David had said, Saul replied, say to David, the king wants no other price for the bride than a one hundred Philistine foreskin. So David took his men out and killed two hundred Philistines and brought back there foreskins" (1 Samuel 18: and 25-27).

"If your hand causes you to sin, cut it off. It is better for you to enter into life maimed, rather than having two hands to go to hell, into the fire that shall never be quenched...

The Forbidden Fruit Or The Forbidden Truth...In The Bible?

If your foot causes you to sin, cut it off. It is better for you to enter life lame, rather than having two feet to be cast into hell, into the fire that shall never be quenched...

If your eye causes you to sin, pluck it out. It is better for you to enter the kingdom of God with one eye, rather than having two eyes, to be cast into hell fire" (Saint Mark 9 and 43-47).

Other hedonistic acts upon the innocence have been perpetrated by zealots of their own beliefs, believing they are/were justified. It Says:

"The king said to the girl, ask me for anything you want, and I'll give it to you, whatever you ask I will give you, up to half of my kingdom. She went out to ask her mother, what shall I ask for? The mother said, The Head of John the Baptist she answers. The girl went back to the king and ask for the head of John the Baptist. The king sent orders to an Executioner, the man went beheaded John in prison and brought back the head on a platter, he presented it to the girl, and she gave it to her mother: (Mark 6 and 22))

"When thy Lord revealed to the angels: I am with you, so make firm those who believe. I will cast terror into the hearts of those who disbelieve. So smite above the necks (behead) and smite every finger-tip of them. This is because they opposed Allah and His Messenger. And whoever opposes Allah and His Messenger then surely Allah is Severe in requiting (judging). Taste it and know that for the disbelievers is the chastisement of the Fire" (Sura 8 and 12-14, Voluntary Gifts).

Rituals and Sacrifices are blamed for the rise of Cultism around the world:

*Jim Jones, of Lebanese decent, created the "Peoples Temple" in which he convinced over nine hundred of his religious follower's cups of cyanide poisoning in 1978.

* Shoko Asahara, form the "Aum Shinrikyo" cult in Japan. In 1994 they unleashed sarin-gas on the subway system in Tokyo Japan.

* Joseph Kibweteere was the leader of the religious movement called "Restoration of the Ten Commandments" in Uganda, Africa. Their mission was to strictly follow the teachings of Jesus. In 2000 he poisoned nearly one thousand of his Ugandan followers.

Dr. Alberto Rivera became a Catholic Priest in 1967. He wrote about the ritual he experienced prior to becoming ordain as a Jesuit Catholic Priest. He wrote, "When a Jesuit of the minor rank is to be elevated to command, he is conducted into the Chapel of the Convent of the Order, where there are only three others present, the principal or Superior standing in front of the altar. On either side stands a monk, one of them holds a banner of yellow and white, which are the Papal colors, and the other a black banner with a dagger and red cross above skull and crossbones, with the word INRI meaning IUSTUM, NECAR, REGES, IMPIOUS, or It is just to exterminate or annihilate impious or heretical Kings, Governments, or rulers. Upon the floor is a red cross at which the postulant or candidate kneels. The Superior hands him a small black crucifix, which he takes in his left hand and presses to his heart, and the Superior at the same time presents to him a dagger, which he grasps by the blade and holds the point against his heart, the Superior still holding it by the hilt, and thus addresses the postulant saying: My son, heretofore you have been taught to act the dissembler; among Roman Catholics to be a Roman Catholic, and to be a spy even among your own brethren, to believe no man, to trust no man.

Among the Reformers, to be a reformer, amongst Calvinist, to be a Calvinist, among other Protestant, and obtaining their confidence, to seek even to preach from their pulpits, and to denounce with all the vehemence in your nature our Holy Religion and the Pope, and even to descend so low as to become a Jew among Jews, that you might be enabled to gather together all information for the benefit of your Order as a faithful soldier of the Pope.

You have been taught to insidiously plant the seeds of jealousy and hatred between communities, provinces, states that were at peace, and incite them to deeds of blood, involving them in war with each other, and to create revolutions and civil wars in countries that were independent and prosperous, cultivating the arts and the sciences and enjoying the blessings of peace. To take sides with combatants and to act secretly with your brother Jesuit, who might be engaged on the other side, but openly opposed to that with which you might be connected, only that the church might be the gainer in the end.

You have been taught your duty as a spy, to ingratiate yourself into the confidence of the family circle of Protestants, amongst the schools and universities, the judiciaries, and councils of states, and to be all things to all men, for the Pope's sake. For without the shading of blood, no man can be saved.

Now in the presence of Almighty God, the Society of Jesus founded by St. Ignatius Loyola, the matrix of God, and the rod of Jesus Christ, declare and swear that his holiness the 'Pope is Christ's Vice-regent and is the true and only head of the Catholic or Universal Church throughout the earth.'

I do further promise and declare to assume my religion heretical, for the propaganda of the Mother Church's interest, by you my ghostly father. I do further promise and declare, that any mental reservation whatever, even as a corpse or cadaver (perinde ac cadaver) but will unhesitatingly obey each and every command that I may receive from my superiors in the Militia of the Pope and of Jesus Christ. That I may go to any part of the world whithersoever I may be sent, to the frozen regions of the North, the burning sands of the desert of Africa, or the jungles of India I will go without repining and I will be submissive in all things." I will address this practice in upcoming chapters.

"However, Mr. Hitchins is remissive, in that he ignored area's where God rejected the sacrifices the children of Israel. It says:

Though you offer Me burnt offerings and your grath (grain) offerings, I will not accept them, nor will I regard your fattened peace offerings. (Amos 5 and 22).

"To what purpose is the multitude of your sacrifices to Me? Says the Lord. I have had enough of burnt offerings of rams and the fat of red cattle. I do not delight in the blood of bulls or of lambs or goats. When you come to appear before Me.

Who has required this from your hand, to trample My courts. Bring no more futile sacrifices; Incense is an abomination to Me" (Isaiah 1 and 11-13).

"O Lord, open my lips, And my mouth shall show forth Your praise. For You do not desire sacrifice, or else I would give it: You do not delight in burnt offering. The sacrifices of God are a broken spirit. A broken and a contrite heart. These, O God, You will not despise" (Psalms 51 and 15-17).

"To do righteousness and justice is more acceptable to the Lord than sacrifice" (Proverbs 21 and 3).

CHAPTER SIX

MOSES, AND THE DESTRUCTION OF KEMIT'S KINGDOM

The story says: "These are the names of the children of Israel who came to Egypt, each man and his household came with Jacob; Reuben, Simeon, Levi, and Judah; Issachar, Zebulun and Benjamin; Dan, Naphtali, Gad, and Asher. All those who were descendants of Jacob were seventy persons for Joseph was in Egypt already. But the children of Israel were fruitful and increased abundantly, multiplied and grew exceedingly mighty; and the land was filled with them" (Exodus 1 and 1-7) After decades of the Israelite people prospering and living freely in the land of Egypt, the Torah writers begin to pivot the narrative into a heinous direction. Making the Pharaoh's antagonistic toward the Israelites and turning them into bondsmen and bondswomen out of envy. So now, the devastation happens to their kingdom would be deem justifiable.

The story says the present King did not know of Joseph. Even though the brothers and wives, and offspring of Joseph's brothers remain in Egypt even after Joseph's death. It says, "Look the people of the children of Israel are more and mightier than we; let us deal shrewdly with them, that they join our enemies and fight against us" (Exodus 1 and 8-10). So this king had foresight that his kingdom would be under attacked when he uttered, "joining the enemies and fight against us." He may have suspected that the Jacobites were becoming operatives and collaborates with the enemies within and outside of Kemit. It is well documented that the Greeks and the Hyksos (Persians) were intertwine with the people of Kemit in their schools, trades, and politics. This king may have seen the writings on the wall of his kingdoms upcoming demise.

The narrative continues saying, the new king "set taskmasters (slave drivers) over them to afflict them with their burdens. And they built for Pharoah supply cities. And they were in dread (fear) of the children of Israel. So the Egyptians, made the children of Israel serve with rigor. They made their lives bitter with hard bondage, in mortar, in brick, and in all the manner of service in the field" (Exodus 1 and 9-15). The Pharaoh gave an edit to two Hebrew midwives to kill all the male children born to their women at birth. But Shiphrah and Puah disobeyed the edit because they had a fear of God. And because of their obedience to God, a home was provided to them. It says, "Therefore God dealt well with the midwives, and the people multiplied and grew very mighty. And so it was, because the midwives feared God, that He provided households for them" (Exodus 1 and 20-21).

My preposition is that it was a western military power in silence, prepared to attack the kingdom of Kemit. Then take control of the dynasty they could never become. This explains the new narrative that is being introduced is that Moses and his people were strangers in Egypt. When they were not. Moses's and his patriarchs travel back and forth, in and out of Egypt, Turkey, and Palestine at will. And they prospered there as well.

Continuing, "Now it happened in the process of time that the king of Egypt died. Then the children of Israel groaned because of the bondage, and they cried out; and their cry came up to God. So God heard their groaning, and god remembered His covenant with Abraham, with Isaac, and with Jacob. And God looked upon the children of Israel, and God acknowledged them" (Exodus 2 and 23-25). Now comes the evolution of Moses and his leadership.

The story says, "And the Angel of the Lord appeared to him in a flame of fire from the midst of a bush, the bush was burning with fire, but the bush was not consumed. Moses said, I will now turn aside and see this great sight, God called to him from the midst of the bush and said, Moses, Moses! Take your sandals off your feet, for the place where you stand is holy ground. He said, I am the God of your father, the God of Abraham, the God of Isaac and the God of Jacob (but Moses father was Amram a bondsman in Egypt), And Moses hid his face, for he was afraid to look upon God. And the Lord said, I have surely seen the oppression of My people who are in Egypt., and had heard their cry because of their taskmasters, for I know their sorrows. So I have come down (from the west) to deliver them out of the hand of the Egyptians, and to bring them up from that land to a good and large land, to a land flowing with milk and honey, to the place of the Canaanites and the Hittites and the Amorites and the Perizzites and the Hivites and the Jebusites. I will send you to Pharaoh that you may bring My people, the children of Israel, out of Egypt" (Exodus 3 and 2-10). I ask, why is it now that bloodshed is the solution, when in the beginning, it was not? Maybe because the once guess, no longer want to be guess, they and their military cohorts determined they should be the new Host.

Let's continue, Prior to Moses return to Egypt as a rescuer; he was hesitant to do so. He said, "When I come to the children of Israel and say to them, The God of your fathers has sent me to you, and they say to me, what is His name? what shall I say to them? God said to Moses, I Am Who I Am, thus you shall say to the children of Israel, I Am, has sent me to you" (Exodus 3 and 13-14). God then said to Moses, "I will stretch out My hand and strike Egypt with all My wonders which I will do in its midst, and after that he will let you go. And I will give this people (not, my people?) favor in the sight of the Egyptians; and it shall be, when you go, that you shall not go empty handed.

But every woman shall ask of her neighbor, namely, of her who dwells near there house, articles of silver, articles of gold, and clothing and you shall put them on your sons and on your daughter. So you shall plunder the Egyptians" (Exodus 3 and 20-22). Meaning, after our military scorch-earth in their cities, we will allow you to loot the dwelling placing of the slain. Just as we allowed you to do when you stole from your father's house in Haran, under Jacob's leadership.

Then God said to Moses, "See, I have made you as God (high ranking officer), to Pharaoh, and Aaron your brother shall be your prophet (lieutenant). You shall speak all that I command you. And Aaron your brother shall tell Pharaoh to send the children of Israel out of his land. And I will harden Pharaoh's ear and multiply My signs and My wonders in the land of Egypt. But Pharaoh will not heed you, so that I may lay My hand on Egypt and bring My armies and My people, the children of Israel, out of the land of Egypt by great judgements. And the Egyptians shall know that I am the Lord, when I stretch out My hand on Egypt (Exodus 7 and 1-5). It's telling you, in rudimentary language that the Lord in this context, is a formidable army, lying in wait to decimate Pharaoh's kingdom. So that they will be a force to acknowledge them as God's after their military victory over them.

These military powers are poetically disguised in the holy books as divine heavenly powers. If they were truly omnipotent entities, they only should express BE! or express BE GONE! and their desires would manifest into existence. God and Lord are the titles selected interchangeably, to replace the human elements of a unified military assembly, position to invade, then rule over the kingdom of Kemit.

But The Holy Quran says, "Every nation has a term. When their term comes, they cannot put it off an hour, nor can they bring it before it's time" (Sura 10 and 49, Jonah). This is why once mighty nations continue to rise on earth, then continue to crumble on earth.

Moses, having the facial recognition of the settlers, then back the Lord and his military forces, Moses is prepared to challenge this new Pharaoh with abundant confidence. It would have been fare-seeming for the hidden enemies of Kemit to select Moses as their operative. The story says, "These are the same Aaron and Moses to whom the Lord said, bring out the children of Israel from the land of Egypt according to their armies. These are the ones who spoke to Pharaoh king of Egypt" (Exodus 6 and 26-27).

They would harden Pharaoh ears, meaning the new king would not unravel the deceptive double talking, double shuffling, and double-dealing intentions of the two, Moses and Aaron. These petty stories of Moses hand turning white as snow; as a sign, rods turning into serpents, rivers and streams, turning into blood, so no one in Egypt could drink from it, were all precursors to their main purpose. The annihilation of Kemit.

The story says, "Thus says the Lord; about midnight I will go out into the midst of Egypt; and all the firstborns of Pharaoh who sits on his throne, even to the firstborn of the female servant, there shall be a great cry throughout all the land of Egypt" (Exodus 11 and

4-6). Then the story takes a pivot. It says, "For I will pass through the land of Egypt on that night and will strike all the firstborn in the land of Egypt, both man and beast; and against all the gods of Egypt I will execute judgement; I am the Lord. Now the blood shall be a sign for you on the house where you are. And when I see the blood, I will pass over you; and the plague shall not be on you to destroy you when I strike the land of Egypt" (Exodus 12 and12-13). You might ask, what does the blood symbolizes, and where does it come from. It says, "Moses called for all the elders of Israel and said to them, pick out and take lambs for yourselves according to your families; and kill the Passover lamb. Strike the lintel and the two doorposts with the blood that is in the basin. And none of you shall go out of the door of his house until morning. For the Lord will pass through to strike the Egyptians, and when He sees the blood on the lintel and on the two doorposts, the Lord will pass over the door and not allow the destroyer to come into your houses to strike you" (Exodus 12 and 21-23). The church teaches that an "angel of death" was sent to perform the sacrifice. However, the storyteller states that the Lord; or the destroyer committed the massacre. The Catholic Church celebrates this day as the "Holy Feast of the Passover."

The day that the Lord of Israel committed infanticide upon a nation of unsuspecting and underserving people. Throughout holy texts, the sacrifice of young males; beginning with the near burnt offering of Abraham's toddler, Isacc in Genesis 22 and 2, and ending with King Herod edit to kill all infant boys, two-years and younger living in Jerusalem, just to prevent the manifestation of the Messiah (Matthew 2 and 1). This practice was viewed as a casual ritual in medieval times. One high ranking official of modern times, named J. Edgar Hoover, in his COINTELPRO program in the 1960's wrote, "there will never be another black messiah, unless we give them one." Meaning, he shall not come from his people, he will be sent to them laced with anti-cooperation sentiments.

I digressed once again. There had to have been other nations suffering from Pharaoh's harsh treatment. It says, "And it came to pass at midnight that the Lord struck all the firstborn in the land of Egypt, from the firstborn of Pharaoh who sat on his throne to the firstborn of the captive who was in the dungeon. So Pharaoh arose in the night, he, all his servants, and all the Egyptians; and there was a great cry in Egypt, for there was not a house where there was not one dead. Then he called for Moses and Aaron by night, and said, Rise, go out from among my people, both you and the children of Israel. And go serve the Lord as you have said. Also take your flocks and your herds, as you have said, and be gone and bless me also" (Exodus 12 and 30-32).

The scribblers do not elaborate on the other people captured living in the dungeons. However, they make another slight reference to them when they wrote, "Then the children of Israel journeyed from Rameses to Succoth. About six hundred thousand men on foot, besides children. A mixed multitude went up with them" (Exodus 12 and 37-38). Rameses is believed to be the name of the Pharoah in charge. A prior verse says, "And Joseph situated his father and his brothers in the land of Egypt, in the best land, in the land of Rameses as Pharoah had commanded" (Genesis 47 and 11-12). Was this mixed multitude the Ethiopians? Notice this verse says the captivity lasted four hundred thirty years. But in a prior chapter, the writers wrote that captivity was only four hundred years. The story continues, "The Lord said to Moses and Aaron, this is the ordinance of the Passover: No foreigner shall eat it. But every man's servant who is bought for money, when you have circumcised him, then he may eat it. And when a stranger dwells with you and wants to keep the Passover to the Lord, let all his males be circumcised, and then let him come near and keep it; and he shall be as a native of the land. For no uncircumcised person shall eat it. One law shall be for the native born and for the stranger who dwells among you.

And it came to pass, on that very same day, that the Lord brought the children of Israel out of the land of Egypt according to their armies (Exodus 12 and 40-51). This verse is interpreted as, only circumcised males were allowed to participate in the Passover. Including all circumcised foreign males who were not of Abraham, Isaac, and Jacob seed, who were also tormented by the Pharaoh's, and who were allowed to exit Egypt with Moses and his people.

Again, who were the foreigners that the writers chose not to reveal? If they were the Ethiopian's, then they were not foreigners. In all actuality, the Ethiopians as well as the Egyptians were related beginning with Abram and Hagar the Egyptian maidservant, and Joseph and his wife Asenath another, Egyptian woman" (Genesis 41 and 44-45). Moses and his wife Keturah the Ethiopian woman. These cultures practice circumcision long before Israel's arrival. I reiterate, the unspoken agenda is to cancel the Egyptian and Ethiopian lineage from the patriarch's ancestry. Their offspring are not foreigners, as described in the text. They were not converted into the bloodline via some "Beit Din" (rabbinical court that determines who becomes a convert to Judaism), or any other mysterious Mikveh (ritual). Instead, they are from the direct seeds of their patriarchs Abraham, Isaac, and Jacob and the rest of the clan.

Prior to 1948, other armies fought against the enemies of the Jacobites. It says, "When you go out to battle (future battles) against your enemies, the Lord your God is with you, who brought you up from the land of Egypt. When you go near a city to fight against it, then proclaim an offer of peace to it. If they accept your offer of peace, then all the people who are found in it shall be placed under tribute (submission) to you and serve you. If the city will not make peace, but war against you, then you shall besiege it. When the Lord your God delivers it into your hands, you shall strike every male in it with the edge of the sword. But the women, the little ones, you shall plunder for yourself. But the cities of these peoples which the Lord your God gives you as an inheritance, you shall let nothing that breathes remain alive, you shall utterly destroy them: the Hittite, Amorite, Canaanite, Perizzite, Hivite, and Jebusite, just as the Lord your God has commanded you" (Deuteronomy 20 and 1-18). The trickery here is to disguise the Children of Israel as the actual soldiers on the battlefield, with the Lord God as their spiritual guidance. But listen to what it says here; "The Lord is my strength. He is my God, and I will praise Him My father's God, and I will exalt Him. The Lord is a man of war; The Lord is His name" (Exodus 15 and 2-4). Who is this man/nation of war that defends the Jacobite's?

Finally, the event that concludes the Exodus story. The children of Israel, and their mixed multitude exited Egypt by crossing the Red Sea. But they were chased by Pharoah's army. The same army that was hit with the seven plagues, then the nationwide infanticide, then dismantled by invading armies. It says, "So the Egyptians pursued them, all the horses and chariots of Pharaoh and his army overtook them camping by the sea beside Pi Hahiroth (near the European-made Suez Canal built to separate Egypt from Arabia and Palestine). The children of Israel cried out to the Lord. Then they said to Moses, because there were no graves in Egypt, have you taken us away to die in the wilderness: Is this not the word that we told you in Egypt saying, let us alone that we may serve the Egyptians? And Moses said, do not be afraid. For the Egyptians you see today, you shall see again no more forever (very true prophecy here. The people in Egypt today are not those of the Ancient Pharoah's. Instead, they are Arabs and Ottomans). The Lord will fight for you. The Lord said to Moses, go forward. But lift up your rod and stretch out your hand over the sea and divide it. And the children of Israel shall go on dry ground through the sea. So I will gain honor over Pharaoh and over all his army, his chariots, and his horsemen. Then the Egyptians shall know that I am the Lord, when I have gained honor for Myself over Pharaoh. And the Angel of God, who went before the camp of Israel, moved and went behind them; and the pillar of cloud went from before them and stood behind them.

So it came between the camp of the Egyptians and that of Israel. Then Moses stretched out his hand over the sea, and the Lord caused the sea to go back by a strong east wind all that night, a mist made the sea into dry land, and the waters were divided. So the children of Israel went into the midst of the sea on dry land ground, and the waters were a wall to them on their right hand and on their left. The Egyptians pursued and went after them. The Lord looked down upon the army of the Egyptians through the pillar of fire and cloud, and He troubled the army of the Egyptians.

And He took off their chariot wheels, so that they drove them with difficulty. They said let us flee from the face of Israel, for the Lord fights for them against the Egyptians (they began to retreat). Then the Lord said to Moses, stretch out your hand over the sea, that the waters may come back upon the Egyptians.

When the morning appeared, the sea returned to its full depth, the Egyptians were fleeing into it. Then the waters returned and covered the chariots and all the army of Pharaoh that came into the sea. Not so much as one of them remained. So, the Lord saved Israel that day out of the hand of the Egyptians, and Israel saw the Egyptians dead on the seashore (Exodus 14 and 9-30). The distance between Rameses and the (man-made) Suez Canal is about two hundred miles. Imagine traveling this distance by foot. With the elderly women and small children included. The same for the livestock they took from the Egyptians. How many of them parish due to scurvy, dehydration, pestilence, and natural death in that desert heat? Nonetheless, the Israelite's landed "in the wilderness of Shur" (Exodus 15 and 22). Shur is located East of Egypt near the Sinai Peninsula. Sinai was called Lower Egypt by the Pharaoh's because of the menial standard of living. The Pharaoh's called the Kingdom of Nubia, which is south of Egypt, Upper Egypt, because of their advanced standard of living. However, both regions were invaded by the Pharaoh's at will. So, the children of Israel never left Egypt. The story describes how they celebrated with songs of how the Lord sank Pharaoh's army in the sea. And how Canaan would fall by the hands of their Lord when they arrived to replace them in their land. But Miriam is named specifically. Who is Miriam? The story says, "Miriam the Prophetess, the sister of Aaron (and Moses) took the tambourine in her hand, and all the women went out after her with tambourines and dances" (Exodus 15 and 20). Miriam gives us another hint of what the Israelite's look like.

What is fascinating is Moses revealed laws from the ten commandments before they were revealed to him. It says, "And they journey from Elim, and all the congregation of the children of Israel came to the Wilderness of Sin (this is a desert named the Valley of Tsin), on the fifteenth day of the second month after they departed from the land of Egypt.

And so, it was on the sixth day that they gathered for each one twice as much bread, two omers (a proportionate amount according to the Egyptian Mathematical Papyrus). Moses then said to them, this is what the Lord has said, "Tomorrow is a Sabbath rest, a holy Sabbath to the Lord. Bake what you will bake today and boil what you will boil, and lay up for yourselves all that remains, to be kept until morning. Six days you shall gather it, but on the seventh day, the Sabbath, there will be none" (Exodus 16 and 1-26). This is the eighth commandment of the ten. How was it that Moses began reciting the rabbinical laws to the congregation, before they were revealed to him by God on the Mountain in Sinai?

Also, notice how the congregation described the condition of slavery they experienced in Egypt, to Moses: It says, "The whole congregation of the children of Israel complained against Moses and Aaron in the wilderness. And the children of Israel said to them, oh, that we had died by the hand of the Lord in the land of Egypt, when we sat by the pots of meat and when we ate bread to the full! For you have brought us out into this wilderness to kill this whole assembly with hunger." These are Astounding revelations made here!

Moses petitioned God to give the congregation something in writing because of their constant and consistent. Thus, the ten-commandment idea germinated after Moses spoke with his father-in-law Jethro, the Ethiopian priest.

The story say's: *Jethro,* the Ethiopian priest, the father of Zipporah, the wife of Moses, came to him and said, "The thing that you do is not good. Both you and these people who are with you will surely wear yourselves out. Listen now to my voice, I will give you counsel, and God will be with you: Stand before God for the people, so that you may bring the difficulties to God. And you shall teach them the statues and the laws and show them the way in which they must walk and the works they must do. You must select from all the people able men, such as fear God, men of truth, hating covetousness, and place them to be rulers of thousands, rulers of hundreds, rulers of fifties, and rulers of tens. If you do this thing, and God so commands you, then you will be able to endure, and all this people will also go to their place in peace. So, Moses heed the voice of his father-in-law and did all that he had said" (Exodus 18 and 17-24). It was Jethro, the Ethiopian priest's idea that Moses gets something in writing that the entire Congregation can adhere too. Moses presented Jethro's thoughts, then God acted.

It continues, "In the third month after the children of Israel had gone out of Egypt, on the same day they came to the Wilderness of Sinai. Moses went up to God. And the Lord called to him from the mountain saying, thus you shall say to the house of Jacob, and tell the children of Israel: you have seen what I did to the Egyptians, and how I bore you on Eagle's wings (America's national emblem) and brought you to Myself. There, if you indeed obey My voice and keep My covenant, then you shall be a special treasure to Me above all people, for all the earth is Mine. And you shall be to Me a kingdom of Priest and a holy nation" (Exodus 19 and 1-6). Moses brought the people out of the camp to meet with God, and they stood at the foot of the mountain.

Mount Sinai was completely in smoke, because the Lord descended upon it in fire. Its smoke ascended like the smoke of a furnace, Moses spoke, and God answered by voice. Then the Lord came down upon Mount Sinai on the top. And the Lord called Moses to the top. And God spoke all these words" (Exodus 19 and 17-25 and Exodus 20 and 1).

The question I want to discuss is what was the true language God spoke on Mount Sinai. The language that the Congregation, and the mixed multitude all understood. And what were the true alphabets God used to write the Commandments? These are the facts that the tomb robbers gloss over in their writings.

I suggest the answer would be Egyptology or Ethiopic. The children of Israel spent more than four centuries of servitude in

Egypt. How could they have kept their native tongue being in bondage for that long? Religious historians boast that the artifacts they discovered were all etched in the Greek lexicon. Unless the Pharaoh's, the Ethiopians, and the Israelites were all Greeks, the entire story of Abraham, Isaac, and Jacob must be the manufacture. The "Kebre Negast," known as the Ethiopian Bible, not only celebrate the rulership of their kings in the Promise Land that the Torah agrees on. It also highlights how the Ark of the Tabernacle exists in their possession to this day. There is one language the Tablets were not carved in, and that was Yiddish. We are all settled on this one.

Moses had to repeat the act of obtaining the Tabernacles from God a second time. The story says, "Moses turned and went down from the mountain (after spending forty days and forty nights the first time), and the two tablets of the Testimony were in his hand. The tablets were written on both sides, on one side and on the other they were written. The tablets were the work of God, and the writing was the writing of God engraved on the tables. It was as soon as he came near the camp, that he saw the calf and the dancing. So, Moses anger became hot, and he cast the tablets out of his hand and broke them at the foot of the mountain. Then he took the calf which they had made, burned it in the fire, and ground it to powder; and he scattered it on the water and made the children of Israel drink it."

Moses then questioned his brother Aaron as to why he instructed the camp to erect the idol Egyptian god to worship? His brother said, "do not let the anger of my lord become hot. You know the people, that they are set on evil.

For they said to me, make us gods that shall go before us; as for this Moses, the man who brought us out of the land of Egypt, we do not know what has become of him. And I said to them, whoever has any gold; let them break it off; so, they gave it to me, and I cast it into the fire, and this calf came out" (Exodus 32 and 15-24). However, Aaron was not forthcoming with his brother. Aaron in fact, was the sculptor of the idol. It says, "Aaron said to them, break off the golden earrings which are in the ears of your wives, your sons, and your daughters, and bring them to me. He receives the gold from their hand, and he fashioned it with an engraving tool, and made a molded calf. Then they said, this is your god O' Israel that brought you out of the land of Egypt! So, Aaron saw it, he built an altar before it. And Aaron made a proclamation and said, Tomorrow is a feast to the Lord" (Exodus 32 and 2-5). By Aaron's silence, he allowed his brother to commit a mass genocide of innocent people in the congregation. It say, "Thus said the Lord God of Israel: Let every man put his sword on his side and go in and out from the entrance to entrance throughout the camp, and let every man kill his brother, every man his companion, and every man his neighbor. So, the sons of Levi did according to the word of Moses. And about three thousand men of the people fell that day" (Exodus 32 and 27-28).

It is fair- seeming that the Levite clan would participate in wanton bloodshed. Their grandfather Jacob cursed them for the bloodshed they committed against the people in Shechem, the city inside of Canaan. Jacob on his death bed said, "Simeon and Levi are brothers; their swords are weapons of violence, let me not enter their council. Let not my honor be united to their assembly: For they have kill men in their anger. Cursed be their anger, so fierce, and their fury, so cruel! I will divide them in Jacob and scatter them in Israel" (Genesis 49 and 5-7). But the Lord has a holy position prepared for Levi and his clan.

Thereafter, the Lord commanded Moses to leave the congregation. It says, "Moses took his tent and pitched it outside the

74

camp, far from the camp, and called it the 'tabernacle of the meeting.' And it came to pass that everyone who sought the Lord went out to the tabernacle of meeting which was outside the camp. When Moses entered the tabernacle, the pillar of cloud descended and stood at the door of the tabernacle, and the Lord talked with Moses. So, the Lord spoke to Moses face to face, as a man speaks to his friend. And he would return to the camp, but his servant Joshua the son of Nun, a young man did not depart from the tabernacle." It gets weird here when the Lord tells Moses and Joshua.

The Lord proclaimed the name of the Lord God, merciful and gracious, longsuffering (patient) and abounding in goodness and truth, keeping mercy for thousands, forgiving iniquity and transgression and sin (even though sin was not known to them because the written laws had not been delivered by Moses), visiting the iniquities of the fathers upon the children and the children to the third and the fourth generation" (Exodus 34 and 6-7). Also, a new name for God was introduced. It says, "For the Lord, whose name is Jealous, is a jealous God" (Exodus 34 and 14). But the name "Jealous" deflects from the divinity, it makes him emotional or having a hypothalamus like us humans. So Jealous God is mentioned only two other times in the holy book. After an additional forty days and nights on top of the mountain, Moses came down and finally delivered the second set of Tablets issued by God.

The story then says, "Then Moses called them, and Aaron and all the rulers of the congregation returned to him, and Moses talked with them. Afterwards all the children of Israel came near, and he gave them as commandments all that the Lord had spoken with him on Mount Sinai. And when Moses had finished speaking with them, he put a veil on his face" (Exodus 34 and 31-33). The veil mentioned here does not represent anything symbolic. At one time, Moses used a veil to cover his shiny face due to scurvies. The story says that

Moses did not eat or drink the entire forty days and nights while on the mountain.

Alan Dershowitz, the sage of modern law today defines the laws in this manner, in his book "The Genesis of Justice": The narratives of injustice that typify the Book of Genesis not only raise the most profound questions about justice in this world and the next, but they also foreshadow many of the specific rules that follow in the Books of Exodus, Leviticus, Numbers, and Deuteronomy. When viewed against the background of the narrative of Genesis, the revelation at Sinai is not the dramatic break with the past that some traditional commentators attribute to it. For Maimonides, prior to Sinai there were no binding laws. But if the Book of Genesis tells the story of the developing legal system ad hoc rules, common law, statues, and so on then, Sinai does not represent so dramatic a break with the past. It is a culmination of a process begun in the Garden of Eden and continued with Cain, Noah, Abraham, Jacob, Dina, Tamar, Joseph, and the other actors in the opening narratives of the Bible. Familiarity with these narratives is a prerequisite to understanding the more formal codes of law revealed at Sinai, since these laws are a rection to the anarchy of the narratives. Many of the laws make explicit or implicit references to narratives, and commentators often tie them together.

To the extent that Sinai does not represent as much of a dramatic break with the past as a culmination of a long process of development, it reflects not only the history of the law, but its historiography as well. We tend to look back at great moments, such as the Magna Carta and the American Constitution, as if they were dramatic breaks with the past. Careful study, however, often discloses that they were actually the inevitable and predictable culminations of developments over time. Because historians crave landmarks and water sheds, they often exaggerate the significance of dramatic singular events that are the culminations of a long, gradual process of adumbration. Magna Carta, for example, summarized and codified developments that were already recognized as part of the common law. Once we had Magna Carta, it became less important to focus on the prior Year Books in order to extract from them the principles that would come to be codified in the great charter. It is to understand that these moments do not arise out of nothingness. In history, there is never a tabula rasa. We always write on a tableau on which much has already been written, erased, and rewritten, even if the tableau is oral. Many traditional commentators disagree, arguing that the Ten Commandments and the other rules emerged full blown from the revelation at Sinai. Jews and Christians number the Ten Commandments differently. For Jews, number one is not even a commandment. The Hebrew for the Ten Commandments is the Ten Statement.

The first statement is a declaration of faith: 'I am the Lord thy God.' It is immediately followed by a summary of the earlier narrative: who brought thee out of the land of Egypt, out of the house of bondage. It could well have continued: into which I placed you by sending Joseph to Egypt and having him summon his brothers and father. After all, this was not the first time God had revealed Himself. He had previously made covenants with Jacob, Abraham, and Noah. Thus, the First Commandment grows directly from the earlier narratives. Christians begin with the theological commandments, 'Thou shalt have no other gods before me.' Thou shalt not make unto thee a graven image, thou shalt not bow unto them or serve them, thou shalt not take the name of the Lord thy God in vain, all of which have their sources in the shift from idolatry to monotheism narrative in the Abraham story. According to midrash (oral interpretation of certain texts), Abraham's father, Terach, was a maker of idols, and one day Abraham then took a hatchet in his

77

hand, and broke all his father's gods, except for the biggest one. When his father saw the smashed idols, he became angry, but Abraham denied breaking them, blaming it on the largest of the idols in whose hand he had planted a hatchet. Terach accused Abraham of lying.

To prove that the large idol had been framed, Terach argues, 'Is there sprit, soul, or power in these Gods? Are they not wood and stone: Have I not myself mad them?' Abraham responded, How, then, canst thou serve these idols in whom there is no power to do anything? Terach then took the hatchet from the hand of the large idol and smashed it. Thus, demonstrating his rejection of false gods, graven images, and idol worship. Hence the commandments against these theological sins.

The Fourth Commandment, 'Remember the Sabbath to keep it holy, derives explicitly from the creation narrative. Indeed, the commandment concludes: For in six days the Lord made heaven and earth, and all that is in them, and rested on the seventh day; wherefore the Lord blessed the Sabbath day and hallowed it.

The Fifth commandment, Honor they father and thy mother, has roots in the stories of dishonor cast upon parents in Genesis. Jacob tricks his feeble father; Shim on and Levi dishonor their father by deceiving and murdering the clan of Shechem; Joseph dishonors his father be deceiving him into sending his youngest son to Egypt; Rachel dishonors her father by stealing his idols and covering up her theft; Cain dishonors his parents by killing their son; Lot's daughters dishonor their father by getting him drunk and raping him; Noah's son dishonors his father by seeing his nakedness and then telling his brother; even Abraham may have dishonored his father by tricking him into giving up his idol worship. Indeed, it can be said that the Book of Genesis is a collection of stories about children dishonoring parents. Clearly, human beings needed a commandment from on high to resolve their intergenerational conflicts.

The Sixth Commandment, thou shalt not murder, has its roots in God's command to Noah, who so shed man's blood by man shall his blood be shed. This rule is derived from another narrative; For in the image of God made He man. The Book of Genesis relates the stories of several murderers and attempted murderers: Cain, Shim'on, Levi, and Abraham. Yet none is punished by death, despite the Noahide covenant. The need for a clear directive is apparent.

The Seventh Commandment, thou shalt not commit adultery, is a bit more difficult to trace directly to a specific narrative. There are, of course, numerous stories of forbidden sex (or at least close calls), Sarah and Rifka with the kings; Lot with his daughters; Tamar with her father-in-law; Reuven with his father's mistress; Potiphar's wife with Joseph, enough to warrant a specific prohibition in the Ten Commandments.

The Eight Commandment, thou shalt not steal, also has roots in the narrative. The midrash traces this prohibition to the Garden of Eden, where God tells Adam: Of every tree of the Garden, thou shalt freely eat: here He commanded him against theft. Adam and Eve violated this command by taking fruit from a prohibited tree. There are other stories of stealing in genesis, including Rachel's theft of her father's idols. Rachel may have believed that it was permissible to steal idols in order to prevent idol worship, an act of religiously motivated civil disobedience akin to the blocking of an abortion clinic, but the commandment is absolute.

The Ninth Commandment, thou shalt not bear false witness against thy neighbor, drives directly from Potiphar's wife bearing false witness against Joseph and Joseph then bearing false witness, even as a pretense against his own brothers. Yehuda's desperate question How can we clear ourselves? Is answered by this prohibition and by the subsequent procedural safeguards that rest on this commandment. Moreover, the earliest biblical narratives support the right of an accused per to a defense, at least against God. God gives Adam and Eve an opportunity to defend themselves and gives Cain the same right. Abraham defends the people of Sodom. God also insists on coming down to earth to see for Himself whether the Sodomites deserve destruction. Hearsay is not good enough even for God. He insists on direct eyewitness observation. But the clan of Shechem is given no opportunity to defend itself against human vengeance. Nor are other victims of human injustice. The need for procedural safeguards against false accusations by human beings is evident.

Finally, the cat-all commandment against coveting one's neighbor's house, wife, manservant, maidservant, ox, ass, nor anything that is thy neighbors, is a general protection against the evil impulses that cause theft, adultery, murder, and the bearing of false witness. The narrative of Genesis is all about these evil impulses and the need to check them by specific rules, laws, and commandments. It was obviously not enough for God to encounter Abraham so that He may command his children and his household after him that they may keep the way of the Lord, to do righteousness and justice. Such generalities had failed to produce an end to lawlessness, deception, and even murder. More specific rules, with prescribed sanctions, were necessary. The narratives of "Genesis made the need for the Ten Commandments, and the laws that followed them, abundantly clear."

"It will continue as long as Adams and Eves are tempted by serpents, Cains are enraged by jealousy, Abraham's fight for justice, Jacobs succeeds by deception, Tamar's are blamed for men's passions, Josephs are falsely accused, and God does not always bring about visible justice. In other words, the story of Genesis will continue until the end of humankind."

A roundtable of theologians believes that the price for "sins" should begin at the period when the written Laws were presented by Moses to his Congregation. And that all acts of egregiousness committed by the congregation should be forgiven, in that the laws were not written down for anyone to follow. Thanks to Jethro, the Ethiopian priest, every nation in the world has its own written laws used to govern their people.

CHAPTER SEVEN
THE FIRST RECORDED CENSUS

Two years after their rescue out of Egypt, "The Lord told Moses to take a Census of all the congregation of the children of Israel, by their families, by their fathers houses, according to the number of names, every male from twenty years old and above, all who are able to go to war in Israel you and Aaron shall number them by their armies" (Numbers 1:1-3). But the house of Levi was to be excluded. It says, "But the Levites were not numbered among them by their father's tribe; for the Lord had spoken to Moses saying; only the tribe of Levi you shall not number, nor take a census of them among the children of Israel; but you shall appoint the Levites over the tabernacle of testimony" (Numbers 1 and 47-50). The Lord wanted to know how many men from Israel were available to war against the Canaanites in their future phantom battle. That number totaled 603,550 potential men of war (even though there are no recorded military records of an Israeli Army defending their interest on a battlefield absent of an advanced Western military power alongside them prior to 1948). The story continues saying that the "tabernacle for meeting" was used as the central point to position their forces. This strategy prepared them to defend or attack their enemies from every direction. The "tabernacle for meeting" was a man-made tent where God met with the Levitical priest to give instructions to the congregation.

To this point, the children of Israel and the mixed multitude are still safe in the Sinai Peninsula. But the moan and groans of mistrust remained an issue. It says, "Now the mixed multitude who were among them yielded to intense craving; so, the children of Israel also wept again, and said, who will give us meat to eat? We remember the fish which we ate freely in Egypt, the cucumbers, the melons, the leek (onions), and garlic; but now our whole being is dried up; there is nothing at all except this manna before our eyes (Numbers 11 and 4-6)! Envy amongst the mixed multitude even rose. It says, "Then Miriam and Aaron (Moses's sister and brother) spoke against Moses because of the Ethiopian woman whom he married (Zipporah, and their son Gershom). They said, Has the Lord indeed spoken only through Moses? Has he not spoken through us also? Suddenly the Lord said to Moses, Aaron and Miriam, Come out, you three to the tabernacle of meetings! Then the Lord came down in the pillar of cloud and stood in the door of the tabernacle and called Aaron and Miriam. Then he said, hear me now My words; If there is a prophet among you, I the Lord make Myself known to him in a vision; I speak to him in a dream. Not so with my servant Moses, I speak with him face to face. Why then were you not afraid to speak against my servant Moses? So, the anger of the Lord was aroused against them, and he departed. And when the cloud departed from above the tabernacle, Miriam became leprous, as white as snow.

So, Aaron said to Moses, oh my Lord! Please do not lay this sin on us, in which we have done foolishly and which we have sinned. Please do not let her be as one dead, whose flesh is half consumed when he comes out of his mother's womb (Numbers 12 and 1-12)! This is a frightening description of how deadly leprosy damages the melanin in the skin.

Aaron was in awe witnessing his sister's swarthy skin tone cursed by God's anger anticipating it did not happen to him. Miriam skin was turned to the same color as her brother Moses hand at the burning bush.

This passage brings forward the question, were the Egyptians, Ethiopian, and children of Israel similar in their appearance? The Prophet Amos alluded to this question when God replied, "Are you not like the people of Ethiopia to Me, O children of Israel?" (Amos 9:7).

So now, after two years of freedom in the Sinai Peninsula, the Lord is assimilating the congregation for this big showdown with the Canaanites for their land. The people who were in object bondage and submissiveness for four centuries are now mentally and physically embolden to engage in a complete take-over of a people their patriarch's knew well. What did they have to do with their enslavement in Egypt? The religious community skips this debate.

The story continues saying, "The Lord spoke to Moses, send men to spy out the land of Canaan, which I am giving to the children of Israel; from each tribe of their fathers, you shall send a man. So, Moses sent them from the Wilderness of Paran (in Sinai), go up to the mountains, and see what the land looks like. Whether the people who dwell in it are strong or weak, few or many; whether the land they dwell in is good or bad, whether the cities they inhabit are like camps or stronghold. Be of good courage. And bring some of the fruit of the land" (Numbers 13 and 1-20). If this was truly an extra-terrestrial power; then Moses and his congregation would have known these answers. However, I suggested that the terms Lord and God are not extra anything. Instead, they were thrones, and kingdoms with superior military powers.

Moses sent Hoshea and Joshua (the one to receive the throne after Moses his death) to spy on the Canaanites. It says, "After spying for forty days, they reported to both Moses and Aaron that we went to the land where you sent us. It truly flows with milk and honey. These two spies went undetected by the settlers in the cities as one of their own.

The people in the land are strong: the cities are fortified and very large; we saw the descendants of ANAK there (ANAK was supposedly a remnant of the Nephilim's mentioned in (Genesis 6 and 2-4), and (Deuteronomy 9 and 2) where it says "a people great and tall, the descendants of Anakim whom you all know, and of whom you heard it said, who can stand before the descendants of ANAK)."

The report said the Amalekites dwell in the land of the south, the Hittites, the Jebusites, and the Amorites dwell in mountains, and the Canaanites dwell by the sea and along the banks of Jordan." It is the territory in the south that modern day Zion specifically targets as their land by inheritance. Even though the story of the "Table of Nations" that Attorney Reverend Bryant reference in opening, said this after the flood; "Now this is the genealogy of the sons of Noah who came out of the ark were Shem Ham and Japhet. The sons of Japhet were Gomer (Ukraine), Magog (Russia), Madai, Javan (Greece), Tubal (Armenia), Meshech (Turkey), and Tiras (France). The sons of Gomer were Ashkenaz (Germans), Riphath, and Togarmah (Eastern Europe today). The sons of Javan were Elishah (Britain), and Tarshis (Spain) Kittim (Rome), and Dodanim (Serbia)" according to the Indian author, Maulana Ali in his book "The Antichrist." "From these the coastland peoples of the Gentiles were separated into their lands, everyone according to his language, according to their families, into their nations" (Genesis 10 and 2-5). These were the families of the sons of Noah, and their generations, in their nations, and by these there were the nations divided in earth after the flood" (Genesis 10 and 1-32).

When the congregation heard these reports, there frustration and indignation of the future of their families in the wild began to spew over. The story says: "So all the congregation lifted their voices and cried, and the people wept that night. And all the children of Israel complained against Moses and Aaron, and the congregation said to them, if only we had died in the land of Egypt! Why has the Lord brought us to this land to fall by the sword, that our wives and children should become victims: Would it not be better for us to return to Egypt? So, they said to one another let us select a leader and return to Egypt" (Numbers 14 and 1-4). Due to the congregations' uncertainties; and resolve to return to their once so-called oppressors; here is what the Lord scheduled for them; "The Lord said to Moses, I will strike them with pestilence and disinherit them, and I will make of you a nation greater and mightier than they, (Moses clapped back at the Lord using his own declaration saying) Then the Egyptians will hear it, for by our might You brought these people up from among them. If you kill these people as one man, then the nations which have heard of Your fame will speak saying,

Because the Lord was not able to bring these people to the land which He swore to give them, therefore He killed them in the wilderness. Just as you have spoken, saying, the Lord is long suffering (patient) and abundant in mercy, forgiving in iniquity and transgression, but He by no means clears the guilty, visiting the iniquities of the fathers on the children to the third and fourth generation. Pardon the iniquity of this people, I pray, according to the greatness of Your mercy, just as You have forgiven this people, from Egypt even until now" (Number 14 and 12-19). Emotions calm down, and the congregation proceeded toward Canaan. As they entered into the Wilderness of Zin, Moses's sister Miriam died and was buried. There was no water there, so the congregation complained to Moses once again, "Why have you brought up the assembly of the Lord into this wilderness? And why have you made us come up out of Egypt, to bring us to this evil place? So, the Lord spoke to Moses saying, take the rod, you and your brother Aaron. Speak to the rock before their eyes, and it will yield its water; thus, you shall bring water for them out of the rock, and give drink to the congregation. Then Moses lifted his hand and struck the rock twice with his rod, and water came out abundantly" (Numbers 20 and 1-11).

Moses was denied entry into the Promise Land by God due to this one act mentioned in this paragraph. Now that the thirst was quenched, Moses requested help from Esau, the twin brother of Israel (Jacob) in Kadesh (Arabia). It says, "Now this is the genealogy of Esau, who is Edom. Esau took his wives from the daughters of Canaan who were descendance of Ham" (Genesis 36 and 1). Here is what Moses inquired of Esau; "Thus says your brother Israel; You know all the hardship that has befallen us, how our fathers went down to Egypt, and dwelt in Egypt a long time, and the Egyptians afflicted us and our forefathers, here we are in Kadesh, a city on the edge of your border. Please let us pass through your country. Then Edom said to him, you shall not pass through my land, lest I come against you with the sword. So, the children of Israel said to him, we will go by the fields and if I or my livestock drink any of your water, then I will pay for it. The he (Edom) said, you shall not pass through. So, Edom came out and attacked them with many men and with a strong hand. So, Israel turned away from him" (Numbers 20 and 14-20). Observe here that the Lord of Israel did not defend them against the Edomites military.

But the congregation began to complain saying, "Why have you brought us out of Egypt to die in the wilderness? For there is no food and no water, and our soul loathes this worthless bread. So, the Lord sent fiery serpents, and they bit the people, and many people of Israel died.

Then Moses prayed to the Lord, the Lord said to him, make a fiery serpent, and set it on a pole (in this instance, Moses was authorized by God to violate His second commandment), everyone who is bitten, everyone who is bitten when he looks at it shall live. So, Moses made a bronze serpent, and put it on a pole; everyone who looked at it lived "(Numbers 21 and 5-9).

Now that the Edomite's refused to allow the congregation access to their land, Moses instead camped on the other side of Arnon. Arnon is the border of Moab, between Moab and the Ammonites (Numbers 21 and 13).

But who are Moab and Ammon? These two nations are descendants of an incestial relationship. It says, "then Lot went up out of Zoar and dwelt in the mountains, and his two daughters were with him (this occurred when Lot and his family escaped Sodom in Arabia), the firstborn daughter said to the younger, our father is old, and there is no man on the earth to come into us as is the custom of all the earth. Come, let us make our father drink wine and we will lie with him, that we may preserve the lineage of our father. So, they made the father drink wine that night.

And the firstborn went in and lay with her father, and he did not know when she lay down or when she arose. If it happen on the next day that the first born said to the younger, let us make him drink wine tonight, and you go in and lie with him. And the younger lay with him, and he did not know when she lay down or when she arose. Both the daughters of Lot were with child. The first born, a son and called his name Moab; he is the father of the Moabites to this day. And the younger, she bore a son and called his name Ben-

88

Ammi; he is the father of the people of Ammon (Ammonites) to this day" (Genesis 19 and 30-38). Modern day Jordan is the territory Moab and Ammon occupied. The two nations refused to allow the Congregation to camp there. And the Ammonites even attack Israel. It says, "Israel defeated him with the edge of his sword and took possession of his land. So, Israel took all these cities of the Ammonites, in Hesborn and in all its villages" (Numbers 21 and 23-35).

The Israelites were able to defeat the Moabites and Ammonites and confiscate all their cities. But they bowed to the Edomites during their attack on them. The question to ask is, what military did Israel ever have? I suggest that Edom and the Edomites were their force of protection, then and now.

A second census was taken while in the land of the Moabites and Ammonites. It says, "the Lord spoke to Moses and Eleazar (son of Aaron); Take a census of all the congregation of the children of Israel from twenty years old and above, all who are able to go to war in Israel.

So, Moses and Eleazar the priest, spoke with them in the plans of Moab by the Jordan, across from Jericho" (Numbers 26 and 1-3). "Now those who were numbered were twenty-three thousand. These are those who were numbered by Moses and Eleazar the priest. But among these, there was not a man who was numbered by Moses and Aaron in the Wilderness of Sinai (Shur). For the Lord had said to them, they shall surely die in the wilderness. So, there was not left a man of them except Caleb and Joshua" (Numbers 26 and 62-65).

Let's analyze this statement. The Congregation had a skirmish with the Edomites at the border of Edom. Then the Congregation just defeated two armies in Jordan. Prior to that encounter, here is what Balak, the King of Moab said, "So Moab said to the elders of

Midian (Ethiopia); Now this company will lick up everything around us, as an ox licks up the grass of the field. Look, a people has come from Egypt. See they cover the face of the earth and are setting next to me! Therefore, please come at once for they are too mighty for me. Perhaps I shall be able to defeat them and drive them out of the land" (Numbers 22 and 4-6). Balak is describing the children of Israel to the Egyptians. A civilization that, that region knows well. It was the Egyptians that provided all of the sustenance to that area when God sent the first plague that crippled that entire region during the days of Joseph. So, how could Moses and the Congregation defend themselves in wartime if their army was destroyed by God in the Wilderness of Shur?

CHAPTER EIGHT

MOSES AT THE END OF HIS ROAD

"The Lord said to Moses; Go up to Mount Abarim and see the land which I have given to the children of Israel. And when you have seen it, you shall gather (lie to rest) to your people as Aaron your brother was gathered. For in the Wilderness of Zin, you rebelled against my command to hollow (venerate) Me at the waters before their eyes (remember, the Lord told Moses to speak to a rock so that it may produce water for the congregation's thirst). Instead, Moses struck the rock with his rod for it to produce the water. His disobedience is known as the "Water of Meribah" rebellion. Then Moses spoke to the Lord, saying set a man over the congregation, who may go out before them and go in before them, who may lead them out and bring them in, that the congregation may not be like sheep's which have no shepherd. The Lord said to Moses; take Joshua with you, a man in whom is the Spirit, and lay your hand on him. Moses did as the Lord commanded. He took Joshua and set him before Eleazer the priest and before all the Congregation" (Numbers 28 and 12-22).

Not that Moses is aware of his faith of not entering the Promise Land that was also promised to him while in Pharoah's house; the Lord is not quite done with him. It says, Moses spoke to the people warning them to fear the Lord their God so that their days may be extended while living in Canaan. It says, "These words which I command you today shall be in your heart. You shall teach them diligently to your children and shall talk of them when you sit in your house, when you walk by the way, when you lie down, and when you rise up. You shall bind them as a sign on your hand, and they shall be as frontlets between your eyes. You shall write them on the doorposts of your house and on your gates. So it shall be, when the Lord your God brings you into the land of which He swore to your fathers, to Abram, Isaac, and Jacob, to give you large and beautiful cities which you did not build, houses full of all good things, which you did not fill, hewn out wells which you did not dig, vineyards and olive trees which you did not plant, when you have eaten and are full, then beware lest you forget the Lord who brought out of the land of Egypt, from fear the Lord your God and serve Him, and shall take oaths in Hie name. When your son asks you in time to come, saying, what is the meaning of the testimonies, the statutes, and the judgements which the Lord our God has commanded you?

Then you shall say to your son, we were slaves of Pharaoh in Egypt, and the Lord brought us out of Egypt with a mighty hand; and the Lord showed signs and wonders before your eyes, great and sever, against Egypt, Pharaoh, and all his household. Then He brought us out from there, that He might bring us in, to give us the land of which He swore to our fathers. Then it will be righteousness for us, if we are careful to observe all these commandments before the Lord our God, as He has commanded us" (Deuteronomy 6 and 6-25). It commands the elders to unabashedly tell their children that

92

their fore-parents were once slaves in this nation. Meaning tell the children how their elder generation was able to conquer the oppression of slavery. This is starchily different from this passage that says, "Then Jesus said to those Jews who believed Him, if you abide in My word, you are My disciples indeed. And you shall know the truth, and the truth shall make you free. They answered Him. We are Abraham's descendants and have never been in bondage to anyone. Jesus said to them, Why do you not understand My speech? Because you are not able to listen to My word. You are of your father the devil, and the desires of your father you want to do. He was a murderer from the beginning, and does not stand in the truth, because there is no truth in him. When he speaks a lie, he speaks from his own resources, for he is a liar and the father of it" (John 8 and 31-44).

The commands continues: It says, "Now the Lord spoke to Moses in the plains of Moab saying; when you have crossed the Jordan into the land of Canaan, then you shall drive out all the inhabitants of the land from before you, destroy all their engraved stones, destroy all their molded images, and demolish all their high places (places of worship, schools, libraries) you shall dispossess the inhabitants of the land and dwell in it, for I have given you the land to possess" (Numbers 33 and 50-53).

The true architects or inhabitants of The Promise Land were to be overthrown and uprooted by superior military powers, without compensation, then for their country to be occupied by an uninvited group of once travelers; now unwelcome aliens.

The anticipation is over, it says, "These are the words which Moses spoke to all Israel on this side of the Jordan in the wilderness. It came to pass in the fourteenth year, in the eleven months, on the first day of the month, that Moses spoke to the children of Israel, on this side of the Jordan in the land of Moab saying, The Lord our God spoke to use in Herob, you have dwelt long enough at this mountain. Turn and take your journey, and go to the mountains of the Amorites, to all the neighboring places in the plain, and in the low land, in the south and on the seacoast, to the land of the Canaanites and to Lebanon, to the great River Euphrates. See I have set the land before you; go in and possess the land which the Lord swore your fathers, Abraham, Isaac, and Jacob to give them and their descendants after them" (Deuteronomy 1 and 1-18).

After that, the Lord said to Moses, "This is the land of which I swore to give Abraham, Isaac, and Jacob, saying, I will give it to your descendants. I have caused you to see it with your eyes, but you shall not crossover there. So, Moses the servant of the Lord died there in the land of Moab. And He buried him in a valley in the land of Moab, no one knows his grave to this day. He was one hundred and twenty years old when he died. The children of Israel wept for Moses in the plains of Moab thirty days. So, the days of weeping and mourning for Moses ended" (Deuteronomy 34 and 4-8). Moses' grave is unknown. Why was Moses grave a mystery?

The book tells where all the progenitors in the past were buried. Including his sister Miriam (Numbers 20 and 1) and his brother Aaron (Numbers 20 and 28). In writings centuries later, the Epistle of Jude implies that Satan inquired about his body for various purposes. It says, "Yet Michael the archangel, in contending with the devil, when he disputed about the body of Moses" (Jude 1 and 9). Why was there a dispute? What was the dispute about? Now Jude speaks of Enoch, he says, "So all the days of Enoch were three hundred and sixty-five years. And Enoch walked with God; and he was not, for God took him" (Genesis 5 and 23-24). So maybe Enoch has the answer. But the writings of Enoch are part of the missing books of the bible. Joshua, Moses's assistant, speaks of Jasher. It says, "Then Joshua spoke to the Lord, is this not written in the Book of Jasher" (Joshua 10 and 12-13)? Maybe Jasher has the answer. But the Book of Jasher did not make the cut either.

Speaking of missing books, Elain Pagels, a Professor of Religious Study at Princeton University wrote in her book "Beyond Belief," "when I entered college, I decided to learn Greek in order to read the New Testament in its original language. Reading these stories in Greek I experienced the gospels in a new way, as if I had never read them before. I entered the Harvard doctoral program. I was astonished to hear that they had files with 'gospels and apocrypha' written during the first centuries which I'd never heard of. These writings containing sayings, rituals, and dialogues attributed to Jesus and his disciples.

Jesus saying, 'For judgement, I came into this world, so that those who do not see may see, and so that those who do see may become blind. I alone offer salvation: All who came before me are thieves and robbers." Professor Pagels goes on to write about the missing books of Thomas, Mary, the Mother of Jesus, of Phillips, and Mary of Magdalene who's scrolls were found in Egypt. She wrote that the Nag Hammadi (this is the name of the city in Kemit where the scrolls were taken by the tomb robbers when they pillaged the libraries there). She describes that "After the Roman emperor Constantine himself converted to the new faith, or at least decriminalized it, did Christian bishops convene in the city of Nicaea, on the Turkish coast, to agree upon a common statement of beliefs the so called Nicen Creed which defines the faith for many Christians." She wrote about the Ebionite Jews, or the Nazarene Jews who were vocal and very present during the Christian movement.

There is a story in the book of Phillip, that he wrote of, "The Lord spoke to Philip saying, Arise and go toward the south which goes down from Jerusalem to Gaza. And behold, a man of Ethiopia, a eunuch of great authority under Candace the queen of the Ethiopians" (Acts 8 and 26-27). The Kebra Nagast supports this notion. It says, "And they blew horns and pipes and trumpets, and beat drums, and sounded all kinds of musical instruments, and there was singing, dancing, games and displays with horses and all the men and women of the country of Ethiopia were present, small and great, and the pygmies, six thousand in number, also virgin women whom Azariah had chosen as the women of Zion whom David the King had destined to serve at the table and the banquets in the royal fortress whenever he went up there clad in raiment of fine gold. So, in this manner was renewed the kingdom of David II (Menyelek I) the son of Solomon the King of Israel, in the capital city Dabra Makeda in the House of Zion, when the Law was established for the first time by the King of Ethiopia. Thuse the eastern boundary of the kingdom of the King of Ethiopia is the beginning of the city of Gaza in the land of Judah and Jerusalem, and its boundary is the Lake of Jericho passing by the coast of its sea to Leba and Saba, bound by Bisis and Asnet. Its other boundary is the Sea of the Black and Naked Men, going up to Mount Kebereneyon into the Sea of Darkness, that is, the place where the sun setteth, extending to Feneel and Lasifala, and its borders are the lands near the Garden of Paradise where there is plenty food and abundance of cattle; this boundary extended as far as Zawel and passeth on to the Sea of India with its boundary as far as the Sea of Taris. In its remote part lieth the Sea of Medyam, until it cometh to the country of Gaza."

Who then was Azariah who is interchangeable spelled Uzziah in the bible? It says, "Now all the people of Judah took Uzziah, who was sixteen years old, and made him king instead of his father

Amaziah. He built Elath and restored it to Judah, after the king rested with his fathers. Uzziah was sixteen years old when he became king, and he reigned fifty-two years in Jerusalem. His mother s name was Jecholiah of Jerusalem. And he did what was right in the sight of the Lord, according to all that his father Amaziah had done" (2 Chronicles 26 and 1-4). Legion has it that Ahaziah was the youngest king to rule Jerusalem. It says, "The inhabitants of Jerusalem made Ahaziah his youngest son King in his place, for the raiders who came with the Arabians into the camp had killed all the older sons" (2 Chronicles and 1). It was the Ebionite Yehuda's ruling in the promise land during the time of the rise of Christianity, plain and clear.

Now back to the Joshua story. Joshua is at the helm now, it says, "When all the kings of the Amorites who were on the west side of the Jordan, and all the kings of the Canaanites who were by the sea, heard that the Lord had dried up the waters of the Jordan from before the children of Israel until we had crossed over, that their heart melted; and there was no spirit in them any longer because of the children of Israel" (Joshua 5 and 1). The story says that the children of Israel began adopting the practices of the settlers whom they just replaced. It says, because they have forsaken Me and made this an alien place, because they have burned incense in it to other gods and have filled this place with the blood of the innocents, they have also built the high places of Baal, to burn their sons (child sacrifice) with fire for burnt offerings to Baal, therefore the days are coming, says the Lord.

"I will make void the counsel of Judah and Jerusalem in this place, and I will make them fall by the sword of their enemies and by the hands of those who seek their lives" (Jeremiah 19 and 4-7). Somewhere in between the death of King David, and his son, King Solomon; the twelve tribes were separated. The tribes of Judah; the son who married the Canaanite woman name Shua (Genesis 38 and 1-6), and the tribe of Benjamin, remained together in the south. Whereas the other ten tribes remain in the northern area of Canaan.

In a revengeful tirade, the Lord said, "Because you have not heard My words, behold, I will send and take all the families of the north, and Nebuchadnezzar the king of Babylon (modern day Iraq) My servant, and will bring them against this land, against its inhabitants, and against these nations all around, and will utterly destroy them and make them an astonishment, a hissing, and perpetual desolations" (Jeremiah 25 and 8-10). So, the Lord is sending one of his servants; King Nebuchadnezzar to topple the children of Jacob, in Israel.

It says, "In the ninth year of Zedekiah King of Judah, Nebuchadnezzar King of Babylon and all his army came against Jerusalem, and besieged it" (Jeremiah 39 and 1). "The army of the Chaldeans pursued the king, and they overtook Zedekiah in the plains of Jericho. All his army was scattered from him. So, they took the king and brought him up to the king of Babylon, and he pronounced judgement on him. Then the king of Babylon killed the sons of Zedekiah before his eyes. He also put out the eyes of Zedekiah and put him in prison until the day of his death" (Jeremiah 52 and 8-11). These are the people whom Nebuchadnezzar carried away captive, in the seventh year, there thousand and twenty-three Jews. In the eighteenth year of Nebuchadnezzar, he carried away captive from Jerusalem eight hundred and thirty-two persons (who were these persons?), in the twenty third year of Nebuchadnezzar, Nebuzaradan, the captain of the guard carried away captive of the Jews seven hundred and forty-five person. All the persons were four thousand six hundred" (Jeremiah 52 and 28-30).

Jeremiah was also taken as prisoner, but King Nebuchadnezzar found favors upon him. He was eventually released from prison. It says, "Then the king commanded Ebed Melech, the Ethiopian, saying, take thirty men with you and lift Jeremiah the prophet out of the dungeon before he dies" (Jeremiah 38 and 10). Once Jeremiah was released, he returned to Jerusalem where a small remnant was spared.

It says, "But Nebuzaradan the captain of the guard left in the land of Judah the poor people, who had nothing, and gave them vineyards and fields at the same time" (Jeremiah 39 and 10).

The questions to ask is, why were the poorest of Judah sparred? It says, "I know your work, tribulation and poverty" (Revelations 2 and 9). The next question is who of the children of Jacob, did the king show mercy to? Were they the two tribes in the south? Meaning the tribe of Judah and Benjamin.

When Jeremiah returned to Jerusalem, he stopped speaking to the Lord. Instead, he and a few others lead Judah back to Egypt in direct defiance of the Lord.

It says, "So Johanan the son of Kareath, all the captains of the forces, and all the remnants of Judah from all nations where they had been driven, men, women, children, the kings daughters, and every person whom Nebuzaradan left behind, and Jeremiah the prophet.

So, they went to the land of Egypt, for they did not obey the voice of the Lord. "Thus says the Lord, the God of Israel, I will bring Nebuchadnezzar, the king of Babylon, my servant, and he will set his throne above these stones. And he will spread his royal pavilion over them, he shall strike the land of Egypt and deliver to death those appointed death, and captivity to those appointed for captivity, and the sword those appointed for the sword.

I will kindle a fire in the houses of the gods of Egypt and shall burn them and carry them away captive. He shall also break the sacred pillars of Beth-Shemesh that are in the land of Egypt; and the houses of the gods of the Egyptians he (Nebuchadnezzar) shall burn with fire" (Jeremiah 13 and 1-13). Beth-Shemesh was a temple erected in ancient Egypt to worship their goddess "Sha-Pash" whom they sometimes prayed to. That worship is characterized as idolatrous in the Torah. However, when Israel occupied Canaan, they erected their own Beth-Shemesh, known as the Temple of the Sun to worship. But their worship is called Holy. It would be fair seeming for the children of Israel to practice in their Egyptian culture with their new culture. Afterall, they lived alongside the Egyptians for four consecutive centuries.

Here, the prophet Jeremiah tells us that a segment of the children of Israel were returned into captivity in the land of the Chaldeans after King Nebuchadnezzar plundered Israel. And another remnant of the children of Israel tells that Jeremiah leads them back to Egypt for their freedom, even in defiance of God. Once in Egypt, Jeremiah is no longer spoken of in the bible. It is believed that Jeremiah died in the land of the Pharaohs in peace. Alongside the remnant of Jews, he rescued.

But now that Egypt is the protagonist in the story, the Lord God became angry with the Pharoah's again. It says, "I will strengthen the arms of the king of Babylon, but the arms of the Pharoah shall fall down; when I put my sword into the hand of Babylon and he stretches it out against the land of Egypt. I will scatter the Egyptians among the nations and disperse them throughout the countries" (Ezkiel 30 and 25). Here the Lord God mentions that Egypt will be scattered amongst the countries after their kingdom falls to Babylon. This must also include the remnant of Jews who escape to Egypt, with Jeremiah, fleeing king Nebuchadnezzars there.

Could it be that this is the missing link that the children of Israel today await? Those Jews Jeremiah returned to Egypt for their safety? It says, "It shall come to pass in that day that the Lord shall set His hand again the second time to recover the remnant of His people who are left, From Assyria and Egypt, from Patho (upper Egypt) and Cush (Ethiopia), from Elam and Shinar (Babylon), from Hamath and the island of the sea" (Isaiah 11 and 11). Is this the honest Forbidden Truth in the bible?

"I believe that Jesus was a Jew. And Jews are not shown in the scriptures to be black persons" is what the Attorney Reverend Bryant proposed in his article to the Times Picayune. Clearly, the Attorney Reverend Bryant lacks Torah, Scriptural, and Talmudic knowledge. Here is some of that knowledge from all three holy books:

Moses said, "My father was a Syrian about to perish, and he went down to Egypt and dwell there, few in numbers; and there he became a nation, great mighty, and populous" (Deuteronomy 26 and 5). The scribbler here is writing about Abraham and not Moses biological father who was Jochebed.

However, the Syrian were interchangeably called Chaldeans in the Torah? It says, "And Terah took his son Abram, and his grandson Lot, and his daughter-in-law Sarai and they left Ur of the Chaldeans to go to the land of Canaan "(Genesis 11 and 31). This passage shows that Terah and his son Abram, Sarai Abram's wife, and his grandson Lot were all Chaldeans from the land of Ur. So, the question I ask, is who are the Chaldeans? It says, "They shall waste with the sword the land of Assyria. And the land of Nimrod at its entrances" (Micah 5 and 6). Then who is Nimrod? It says, "Cush (Ethiopia) begot Nimrod; he began to be a mighty one on the earth. He was a mighty hunter before the Lord. And the beginning of his kingdom was Babel, Erech, Accad, and Caineh, in the land of Shinar. From that land he (Nimrod) went to Assyria and built Nineveh, that is the principal city" (Genesis 10 and 8-12). According to Torah, Nimrod, the grandson of Ham, was the father of the Chaldeans. And not Shem as mentioned in Genesis 11. Let's discuss at length, who Nimrod: Legion says that "In the Lord's eyes," does not mean that the Lord found favor in his hunting abilities. History shows that Nimrod and the kingdom he built were hunters of human life and large land mass. And not the hunter of animals as God assigned Esau to become. Nimrod was the father of Babel or Babylon and three other cities. He erected his kingdom inside of a kingdom that already existed called Shinar. Shinar is connected with Nimrod's kingdom in various other texts and has done so with malicious intent.

For example, the story of the two women concealed in a basket is linked to Nimrod. It says, "Then I raised my eyes and looked, and there were two women, coming with the wind in their wings, for they had wings like the wings of a stork, and they lifted up the basket between earth and heaven. So, I said to the angel who talked with me, Where are they carrying the basket? And he said to me To build a house for it in the land of Shinar, when it is ready, the basket will be set there on its base: (Zechariah 5 and 9-11). Nimrod's kingdom was also the one the Lord called on to defeat his children, after they arrived in Jerusalem due to their wickedness. It says, "Jeremiah the prophet spoke to all the people of Judah and to all the inhabitants of Jerusalem, saying, Thus says the Lord, Nebuchadnezzar the king of Babylon, My Servant, will bring them against this land, against its inhabitants, and against these nations all around, and will utterly destroy them, and make them an astonishment, a hissing, and perpetual desolations" (Jeremiah 25 and 2-9). Nimrod's kingdom was called by God to defeat the Egyptians for courting the remnants of Israel whom Jeremiah and Baruch rescued from burning Jerusalem. It says, "I will send and bring Nebuchadnezzar the king of Babylon, My Servant, and will set his throne above these stones that I have hidden. And he will spread his royal pavilion over them. When he comes, he shall strike the land of Egypt and deliver to death those appointed for death, and to captivity those appointed for captivity, and to the sword those appointed for the sword" (Jeremiah 43 and 10-11). Nimrod just as all of the Pharaoh's in the Pentateuch, are the focal point of the patriarch's history. Abram was a Chaldean. Moses was a Chaldean. Jochebed was a Chaldean. Terah was a Chaldean. The Hebrew's were Chaldeans. And they were all descendants of Ham! Not of Japheth. And not of Shem. Here are a few written signs of who the children of Israel in the Genesis story came from: The Gospel says, "an angel of the Lord appeared to Joseph in a dream, saying, Arise, take the young Child and His mother, flee to Egypt, and stay there until I bring you work; for Herod will seek the young Child to destroy Him. When he arose, he took the young Child and His mother by night and departed for Egypt, and was there until the death of Herod, that it might be fulfilled which was spoken by the Lord through the prophet, saying, Out of Egypt I called My Son" (Matthew 2 and 13-15).

The prophet Saint Matthew referred to is found in the Septuagint. It is written in the book of Hosea. It says, "When Israel was a child, I loved him, and called him out of Egypt" (Hosea 11 and 1).

The Babylonian Talmud, tells the same story, it says:

"The Gemara ask, To where did Sennacherib (ancient Chaldean empire) exile the ten tribes: Mar Zutra (a Babylonian Rabbi) says, He found them in AFRICI" (Sanherin: 94a).

Back to the story, Moses's foresight showed him a disastrous future for the children of Israel once they entered into the land of Canaan. He saw that they would return into back into bondage in ships to a nation far away.

That they would be sold as slaves to a mighty nation far away. That they would serve other gods which neither them nor their fathers heard of, wood and stone.

And become a proverb (a pity) and a byword (notorious) among all nations where the Lord will drive them.

While in those nations, they would find no rest, nor soles for their feet, but will have a trembling heart, failing eyes, and anguish of soul.

That their life would hang in doubt before them; they would be afraid day and night and would have no assurance of life. The mornings they shall sing Oh if it was evening, and at evening, you shall say Oh that it was morning! Because of the fear that would terrify their hearts (minds), and the unending terror their eyes see.

While there, they would betroth a wife, but another man would lie with her at his convenience, that their sons and daughters would be sold to other people in front of their eyes, and there would be no strength left in their hands, that a nation whom they would not know would eat the fruits of their land and the produce of their labor, and they would only be oppressed and crushed continually.

That they would be driven mad because of the sight which their eyes shall see. While there, they would put a yoke of iron on their neck until He has destroyed you.

While there, the alien (immigrants) who is among them shall rise higher and higher above you, and you shall come down lower and lower. He shall lend to you, but you shall not lend to him.

The Lord will bring this nation against you from afar, from the end of the earth, as swift as the Eagle flies, a nation whose language you will not understand, a nation of fierce countenance which does not respect the elderly nor show favor to their young. This is the vision Moses was given in Jericho before his people crossed over into the Promise Land (Deuteronomy 28 and 30-68).

In May of 1948, more than two thousand years later, Israel became a nation, with the aide and governance of the West. It is established in the ancient territory of Palestine. However, Henry Ford, the Motor magnate, and author of "The International Jew," wrote in his book, "At the Sixth Congress the British government had offered the Jews a colony in Uganda, East Africa. Herzl was in favor of taking it, not as a substitute for Palestine, but as a step toward it." As the days of old, the Ugandan settlers would not have had a vote on their opinion of a new colony occupying their nation. And neither did the settlers in Palestine.

This author has made several insinuating opinions on the matter of Jewishness. He wrote, "At the present time, if any government raises a protest against us, it is only for the sake of form, it is under our control, and it is done by our direction, for their antisemitism is necessary for keeping in order our lesser brothers. I will not explain this further as it has already been the subject of numerous discussions between us. This doctrine of the usefulness of antisemitism and the desirability of creating it where it does not exist and found in the words of Jewish leaders, ancient and modern. In reality there are no obstacles before us. Our super government has such an extra-legal status that it may be called by the energetic and strong word...dictatorship. I can conscientiously say that at the present time we are the lawmakers. In that Protocol this claim is made: 'De-facto, we have already eliminated every government except our own, although de jure there are still many others left. That is simple; the governments still exist, under their own names, having authority over their own people; but the super-government has unchallenged influence over all of them in matters pertaining to the Jewish Nation and particularly in matters pertaining to the purpose of the "The International Jew." The Eight protocol show how this can be: For the time being, until it will be safe to give responsible government positions to our brothers Jews, we shall entrust them to people who's past and whose character are such that there is an abyss between them and the people to people, for whom, in case of disobedience to our orders, there will remain to their last breath. In the Ninth protocol again is this reference to party funds: as in order to carry on a party struggle it is necessary to have money, and we have it all." But Mr. Ford harbors more incendiary beliefs that he never justified in his book. He says, "To make a list of the lines of business controlled by the Yehudah's of the United States would be to touch most of the vital industries of the country. Those which are really vital, and those which cultivated habit has made to seem vital. The theatrical business, of course, as everyone knows, is exclusively Yehudah's. Play-producing, booking, theater operation is all in the hand of Yehudah's.

This perhaps accounts for the fact that in almost every production today can be detected propaganda, sometimes glaringly commercial advertisement, which does not originate with playwrights, but with producer.

- The motion picture industry
- The sugar industry
- The tobacco industry
- Fifty per cent or more of the meat packing industry
- Upward of 60 per cent of the shoemaking industry
- Men's and women's ready-made clothing

- Most of the musical purveying done in the country
- Jewelry
- Grain
- More recently, cotton
- The Colorado smelting industry
- Magazine authorship
- New distribution
- The liquor business
- The loan business

These, only to name the industries with national and international sweep, are in control of the Yehudah's of the United States, either alone or in association with Yehudah's overseas." What I find remarkable, is that Mr. Ford did not list any of the automobile making manufactories that he monopolizes. Both in the United States and overseas.

The author Louis Rapport wrote of the Falasha Ethiopian Jews brought into Israel in the 1970's this, "The Falasha's were rediscovered by world Jewry in the 19th century when it seemed certain that Protestant missionaries from England would convert the Ethiopian Jews, and that the tribe would assimilate and disappear. The Jewish-Christian struggle over the Beta-Israel was to have a profound effect on the tribe's fate. The nature of the religious struggle has prejudiced research on the Beta-Israel by interested parties from both sides. As Wolk Leslau noted in his Falasha Anthology: 'Most of the reports that have so far been made about the Falasha's are incomplete and characterized by a Christian or Jewish missionary tendency which appreciably diminishes their value.'

Jesuits preceded the Protestants to Ethiopia by three hundred years, accompanying Portuguese soldiers into the country in 1541.

The Jesuits charged that there was a dangerous Hebraic mold to the Abyssinian Christian church, which was founded in the fourth century when a shipwrecked Syrian Christian converted the Ethiopian ruler (the falsehood has to be exposed. The Abyssinian Christian Church was established by the Ethiopian Jews prior to this ridiculous shipwreck farce). The Jesuits had some initial success, but their political meddling enraged the Abyssinian priest and by the middle of the 17th century, the Society of Jesus was banished from Ethiopia. There were no more Christian missionaries from the west until the 19th century colonial ear, when the great explores were followed by waves of missionaries, soldiers and merchants (those were colonizers sent to the region to erase the ancient historical history of the Ethiopian Jews along with vandals and looters). Explorer James Bruce's encounter with the Falasha's at the end of the 18th century was to inspire a movement of British missionaries, pious Anglicans, who read his popular travel account and vowed to convert the Abyssinian Jews. The protestant crusade began in 1809 with the founding of the London Society for the promotion of Christianity Amongst the Jews, which aimed at converting the Jew of Africa. Samuel Gobat, who first sought out the Beta-Israel in 1830, would become the inspirational leader of the movements effort to win over the Beta-Israel. Gobat, who later became Anglican bishop in Jerusalem, worked with several German-Jewish converts to Protestantism, including the Reverends Wolff, Isenberg, Rosenthal and the most fanatical of them all, Henry A. Stern. In 1855 Gobat sent two missionaries from Jerusalem to Ethiopia to obtain permission from emperor Theodore to convert the Falasha's. The emperor told missionaries J.F. Krapf and J.M. Flad that he was willing, but only if the Jews were baptized into the Ethiopian Orthodox Church.

Another outside observation of the Jewishness of Ethiopia people, although similar to Louis Rappoport's book, is an article published by Rabbi Sholomo Levy. He implies that many of the African ancestry does not, or will not adhere to the Talmud teachings. He says, "The practices of the Beta Israel differ significantly in some areas from those of other forms of Judaism. Since in Ethiopia, the Beta Israel community was for the most part unaware of the Talmud. They did, however have their own Oral Law. However, their religious elders, or priestly class, interpreted the Biblical Law of the Tenak in a not completely dissimilar way to that used by other rabbinical Jewish communities in other parts of the world. In that sense, the Beta Israel had an analogous tradition to the Talmud, although at times at variance with the practices and teachings of other Jewish communities throughout the world. Today, they are a community in flux; some of them accept normative Judaism, (i.e., the rabbinic/Talmud tradition that is practiced by other Orthodox Jews, and many of the younger generation of Ethiopian Israelis have been educated in yeshivas (colleges or seminaries) and received rabbinical semicha (laying of hand), while a certain segment of traditionalist Beta Israel insists on maintaining their separate and distinct form of Judaism as practiced in Ethiopia and Eritrea. Many of the Ethiopian Jewish youth who have immigrated to Israel have assimilated to the dominant form of Orthodox Judaism as practiced in Israel, while others have assimilated to a secular lifestyle in Israel. One significant difference is that they lack the festivals of Purim and Hanukkah. This might be because they branched off from the main body of Judaism before these holy days were developed."

In short, what this Rabbi is attempting to explain; is that Lineage supersede all ritual and agreed upon practice. The Ethiopian Jews are who they are by heritage. This Rabbi and his congregation are who they are, by written practices published in a Talmud. A book of fables agreed upon by Rabbinic scholars throughout the centuries. However, since they are closely connected to the western dominance, their oral tradition is the deciding factor in Jewelry today. The Ethiopian Jews pre-dates their Talmud's. They did not need one. They are what is recorded in the Talmud. Rabbi Levy mentioned the phrase "before they branched off from the main body of Judaism," but he did not dwell on that topic. The following passages will introduce you to one form of branching off, sent in the guise of Missionaries, and how they sabotage the family tree.

The Protestant felt that this provision was not much of a concession. On the contrary, they believed that the arrangement would provide a means for reforming Ethiopian Christianity from within. Theodore gave his full support to the Church Mission to the Jews, since the emperors had been trying for centuries to convert the Falasha's. One of his first gestures to the Protestants was to ban the Beta-Israel practice of animal sacrifice. The missionaries registered further progress in 1860, when henry Stern left his mission work in the Middle East and set out to bring the Gospel of Christ to the Falasha's, He was ordained in Jerusalem by another apostate Jew, Bishop Michael Solomon Alexander. Stern was a quixotic Christian soldier who had labored hard to win Jewish souls in Arabia, Turkey, Baghdad and Persia. He was bent on bringing evangelical Protestantism to jews in the remotest areas of the earth, spurred, perhaps, by his own apostasy. In 1859 the Lonon Society provided funds for Stern to conduct an intensified mission to the Ethiopian Jews. Stern kept a rather anemic account of his Ethiopian adventures, sketching only his reception by Emperor Theodore and his visits to Falasha villages but going into depth when recounting his proselytizing speeches to the natives. His book, Wanderings Among the Falasha's in Abyssinia, was aimed at an English audience hungry for information about the exotic black Jews of deepest Africa. Stern went back to England after only a few months in Ethiopia and got on the lecture circuit to raise more money for the mission. Meanwhile, his colleagues in Ethiopia were baptizing their first Falasha converts (at the barrow of their muskets) in 1862. Stern would return that year with two reinforcements: fellow German Jewish Converts, Reverend Henry Rosenthal and his wife. The missionaries were not always prepared for the work ahead of them. Two English travelers in Sudan during the time described their meeting near the Ethiopian border with two German born missionaries from England: The missionaries had brought with them trunks full of Christian Bibles printed in Tigre (Eritrea today), which neither they nor the Falasha's could read, and they carried a large supply of medicine that they did not know how to administer. Henry Stern made definite headway in this second journey. He soon appointed converted Falasha's as lay preachers, and he sent them out to the villages. New converts were duly baptized into the Ethiopian church, in accordance with the agreement between the emperor and this practice was still being followed by the mission in the 1970's."

He goes on to write, "the Italians were defeated at Adowa, Emperor Menelik II (heir son of king Solomon and Sheba) encouraged the Falasha (Christian) converts to reopen the Christian Mission of the Jews missions, which prospered until the next Italian invasion of Ethiopia two generations later. The Italians allowed only Catholic missionaries to work in Ethiopia during their six-year occupation, 1936-1942. But after World War II, Emperor Haile Selassie resumed wholehearted support of the London Society for Promoting Christianity Amongst the Jews, and he welcomed back the exiled Protestant missionaries. In recent years, the church mission and a rival Seventh Day Adventist mission to the Falasha's still used converted Falasha's to preach to fellow tribesmen, and proudly boasted that there were many Hebrew Christians in the field on four continents. In pamphlets put out regularly during the last one hundred years, the mission has promised to break down the strong holds of Satan, the dark prince who makes the Jews of Christendom oppose the Messiah of the New Testament" (pay attention to what Louis Rapoport is describing. He is describing how the West sent Catholic Priest and Christian Missionaries to those regions of the world to erase their Hebraic/Judaic legacy, culture, and beliefs by goading them to accept their Jesus analogy. While simultaneously allowing the converted Yehudah's in Israel, which was once ruled by Ethiopian Kings, to remain free to practice their newly converted faith in Judaism). He continues; "A church comic book, Abyssinian Adventure, features a converted Falasha boy who is determined to 'win my people for Jesus Christ' even though he recognizes that this will bring discord, strife, it may be, even the shedding of blood. It has been so in all ages of the Church. The missionaries are a dedicated lot; many of them spent ten, twenty or more years working in Ethiopia. In Eric Payne's missionary book, Ethiopian Jews, two characteristics of the missionaries are described; the resolve to identify with the Falasha's and the resolve to endure the hardship of life in Ethiopia. Payne himself was an Englishman with a curacy in Bath when he heard God's call and was overwhelmed by the need to take the Gospel to the Jews (in Africa, but not in Israel). Payne was distressed in 1954 when Israel established 35 schools for the Beta-Israel in Begembdar province. He felt that his prayers were answered when Israeli doubts about the Falasha's Jewishness finally prevailed: Israel stopped sending any more grants. By 1958, there were only a few village schools left. Payne was relieved that the Orthodox Jewish rabbis in Israel have rejected the Falasha's. To his mind, the mission was doing nothing but good for the Falasha's, and the Israelis had threatened to delay the advance of Christianity in remote northwest Ethiopia."

Here we have the nineteen-century old Hebraic/Judaic culture of the Ethiopian people being decided by an Englishmen's bigoted beliefs of the direction he thinks they should be led to believe. He continues, "Anthropologist Michelle Schoenberger holds a different view of the mission's effect on the Beta-Israel. She asserts that a Falasha who converts sells himself for a mess of pottage: 'When a Falasha converts to Christianity, he believes, or rather has been led to believe, that when he is baptized into the Church and has agreed to follow the teachings of Jesus Christ, he will lose the stigma which is attached to his Falasha heritage. He also believes that he will become an Amhara after his baptism and so he will be able to marry an Amhara (part Ethiopian and Asiatic) girl and thereby receive rights to land through his Amhara wife'. But he always remains just a baptized Falasha to the Amhara. He's never accepted, and he'll rarely find an Amhara woman willing to marry him. Furthermore, his fellow tribesmen will have nothing to do with him. The convert is excommunicated, left in missionary limbo. The missionaries, of course, saw themselves as divinely inspired idealists, bringing civilization and God and law to the natives: Indians, Africans, Chinese, Jews. Many of them have viewed their work as a Christ-fight against Muslims missionaries, for Islam has steadily been winning Africa."

Ancient scholars wrote about the prosperity of the Palestine territory. The Greeks called them Phoenicians. They described them as a Hamitic nation of people who lived along the shores of Lebanon. The Phoenicians were large trading partners with the Greeks. However, they should not be mixed with the Syro-Phoenicians who were a mixed-race people with both Hamitic and

Syrian background during the time period of the Roman conquest. They Syro-Phoenician's are mentioned in the Gospel of Mark 7:28.

Louis Rappoport describes merely a tiny fraction of the methods perpetrated by western authoritarians that contributed to the annihilation of a people and culture that pre-date the Christ anthologies. Moses saw this destruction, then replacement of his people in a vision he had, as he stood on the plains of Mount Nebo in Jericho, just prior to the children of Israel crossing the Jordan River into the Promise Land: He envisioned that they would serve gods, at the work of men's hands, which neither them nor their fathers heard of, wood (the cross) and stone (mecca) in Deuteronomy 4 and 28. Moses envisioned that his Congregation would eventually be replaced by a nation of Beit Din converts who are closely aligned to the powers of the western dominance rulers. Moses saw that by him leading the children of Israel out of the land that he was sheltered in, the land that his ancestors prospered in, the land that Jeremiah returned a remnant of the family to, was a suicidal move on his part.

CHAPTER NINE
"GOD CURSED HAM, AND HAM WAS BLACK," HE WROTE

In the chapter called "The Opening," the Attorney Reverend Bryant expressed in his article to the Times Picayune in New Orleans, that the black race is cursed by God through the sins of Ham, their father, and that is why Jesus cannot be a black person. The Reverend did not address that part of his letter to the editor during his opening. And he refused to comment about it when questioned by his opponent Dr Khalid.

Talmudist, Evangelical Preachers, Mormonist, and institutes of esteem learning, policy makers of heads-of-states have supported this folklore to the demise of their own souls. The bestselling author and legal sage, Alan Dershowitz, a Yahuda, wrote in his book "The Genesis of Justice" that "an imaginative midrash says that Ham attempted to perform an operation upon his father designed to prevent procreation. Rashi suggests that Ham indulged a perverted lust upon him, thus Ham's descendants were cursed." Louis Rapoport, another renowned Yehuda wrote in his book "The Lost Jews" that "the sons of Ham children were cursed because of their father's transgression, the lowest of slaves to his brothers, the Sin of

Ham." This popular Babylonian-Talmudic story crept its way into the Torah, and Christian literature centuries ago.

Other legions go further saying, Ham was cursed with black skin in the Ark for having sexual intercourse during the flood. Here is what the Tenak says regarding that; "on the very same day Noah, and Noah's sons, Shem Ham, Japheth, and Noah's wife, and three wives of his sons with them entered the ark" (Genesis 7 and 13). The legion does not state if his relationships may have been with his wife. It certainly does not site the other family members behavior on the Ark, because that would diminish the rage against the Hamitic people that the legion was written to embarrass.

Another story is that Ham had red eyes because he saw Noah naked in a drunken stupor, then made fun of him. But this is what Tenak say about Israel, "Until Shiloh (King David) comes, His eyes shall be red than wine" (Genesis 49 and 10-12). Was Israel excommunicated due to his red eyes?

Now here is what the Torah story says, "Now the sons of Noah who went out of the ark were Shem, Ham, and Japheth. And Ham was the father of Canaan (why is Ham and his unborn child Canaan targeted from the onset)? These three were the sons of Noah, and from these the whole earth was populated. Noah began to be a farmer, he planted vineyard. He drank the wine and was drunk and became uncovered in his tent.

And Ham, the father of Canaan saw the nakedness of his father and told his two brothers outside. But Shem and Japheth took a garment, laid it on both their shoulder and went backward and covered the nakedness of their father. Their faces were turned away and they did not see their father's nakedness. Noah awoke and knew what his younger son (that would be Japheth, not Ham) had done to him. Then he said: Cursed be Canaan A servant of servants, He shall be to his brethren" (Genesis 9 and 18-26). Yet another legion suggests that Ham had committed an indecent and unlawful carnal act against Noah in the tent. But Noah remained asleep. Any crime of that nature would have awoken Noah.

The attacks are relentless. Another legion is that Ham entered the tent of his mother Naamah and had incestuous relation with her while Noah was asleep in his tent (the Tenak suggest that Naamah, the sister of Tubal-Cain was the wife of Noah Genesis 4 and 22). The question I ask is why is Naamah so hidden in the Tenak? Afterall, she is allegedly the "Mother" of all the Semitic, Hamitic, and Japhetic nations of people. When Noah did awake, that is when he chastised Ham, then cursed his unborn nephew Canaan. But Noah was not given divine power by God. For example, it says of Moses, "God made Moses appear as a God to Pharoah" (Exodus 7 and 1). Noah was not blessed with that kind of power. Whatever disgust Noah displayed; it would not mount to him having the authority to issue any punishment to an unborn child. Especially if that punishment was to last into perpetuity. Noah would have had equal power as the Lord God who created the world in six days, then flooded it in forty days. It says, "The soul who sins shall die. The son shall not bear the guilt of the father, nor the father bear the guilt of the son. The righteousness of the righteous shall be upon himself, and the wickedness of the wicked shall be upon himself" (Ezekiel 18 and 20).

Let's remember the Attorney Reverend Bryant wrote "God cursed Ham" in his letter to the editor. The story says that the sons of Ham were Cush (Ethiopian), Mizraim (Egyptians), Phut (Libyans), and Canaan (Palestinians). The kingdom of these nations of people stands front and center throughout the Old Testament text due to the land they inherited after the flood. The Table of Nations outlines the geographical areas on earth that the sons were positioned by God to populate. It says, "These were the families of the sons of Noah, according to their generations, in their nations, and from these the nations were divided on the earth after the flood" (Genesis 10 and 32). Every nation of Ham's so-called descendants was attack, striped of their land, minerals and resource at the hands of his brothers' (Shem, Japheth) and their descendants.

Back to the Naamah story. The Levites had in place specific rules about uncovering family members nakedness. It says, "None of you shall approach anyone who is near of kin to him, to uncover his nakedness. The nakedness of your father or the nakedness of your mother you shall not uncover. These are the two violations they want to charge Ham of violating.

She is your mother; you shall not uncover her nakedness. The nakedness of your father's wife you shall not uncover. You shall not uncover the nakedness of your father sister; she is near of kin to your father. You shall not uncover the nakedness of a woman and her daughter, nor shall you take her son's daughter or her daughter's daughter, to uncover her nakedness, you shall not take a woman as a rival to her sister, to uncover her nakedness while the other is alive" (Leviticus 18 and 6-17). It latter says, "Every one of you shall revere his mother and his father" (Leviticus 19 and 3).

Now with this said, there were multiple times when the children of Israel engaged in relations that they ruled immoral. The Lord God of Abraham, Isaac, and Jacob nor their descendants were ever chastised for those transgressions.

Let's look at a few; Lot's two daughters' incestuous relationship with their father. Two sons were borne, they named them Moab and Ammon.

Jacob first sleep with Leah, the daughter of Laban, then he slept with her sister Rachel, then he slept with both their maidservants,

Zilpah and Bilhah, while thy were alive. It says, "Leah conceived and bore a son, and she called his name Reuben." Then she gave him Bilhah her maid as wife, and Jacob went in to her. And Bilhah conceived and bore Jacob a son. When Leah saw that she had stopped bearing, she took Zilpah her maid and gave her to Jacob as wife. And Leah's maid Zilpah bore Jacob a son" (Genesis 30 and 3-10). Here we see that Jacob was awarded a windfall for his prowess. Not only did he get two sisters, but he got both their maidens as an unexpected gift.

Reuben, went and lay with Bilhah, his father's concubine, and Jacob heard about it (Genesis 35 and 22). He did not receive generational chastisement as did Canaan for the exact violation, allegedly. It says, "Now the sons of Reuben the first born of Israel, he was indeed the firstborn, but because he defiled his father's bed, his birthright was given to the sons of Joseph, the son of Israel, so that the genealogy is not listed according to the birthright" (1 Chronicle 5 and 1).

Even though Jacob had married a Canaanite woman name Shua. Jacob laid with Tamar, another Canaanite woman he took to marry his son Er. Jacob then impregnated her with two sons. They name them Perez and Zerah. It says, "Then Judah took a wife for Er, his firstborn, and her name was Tamar. But Er, Judah's firstborn, was wicked in the sight of the Lord, and the Lord killed him. Then Judah said to Tamar his daughter-in-law, 'Remain a widow in your father's house till my son Shelah is grown. For he said, lest he also die like his brothers, And Tamar went and dwelt in her father's house. Now in the process of time, the daughter of Shua, Judah's wife died; and Judah was comforted, and went up to his sheep shears at Timnah, he and his friend Hirah the Adullamite. And it was told Tamar, saying, Look, your father-in-law is going up to Timnah to shear his sheep. So she took off her widow's garments, covered herself with a veil and wrapped herself, and sat in an open place which was on the way to Timnah; for she saw that Shelah was grown, and she was not given to him as a wife. When Judah saw her, he thought she was a harlot, because she had covered her face. Then he turned to her by the way, and said, Please let me come in to you; for he did not know that she was his daughter-in-law. So, she said, 'What will you give me, that you may come in to me?' And he said, I will send a young goat from the flock. So, she said, Will you give me a pledge till you send it? Then he said, What pledge shall I give you? So, she said, 'Your signet and cord, and your staff that is in your hand'. Then he gave them to her, and went in to her, and she conceived by him. So, she arose and went away, and laid aside her veil and put on the garments of her widowhood. And Judah sent the young goat by the hand of his friend the Adullamite, to receive his pledge from the woman's hand, but he did not fine her. Then he asked the men of that place, saying, Where is the harlot who was openly by the roadside? And they said, There was no harlot in this place. So, he returned to Judah and said. I cannot find her. Also, the men of the place said there was no harlot in this place. Then Judah said, Let her take them for herself, lest we be shamed; for I sent this young goat and you have not found her. And it came to pass, about three months after, that Judah was told, saying, Tamar your daughter-in-law has played the harlot; furthermore, she is with child by harlotry. So Judah said, 'Bring her out and let her be burned!' When she was brought out, she sent to her father-in-law, saying, By the man to whom these belong, I am with child, and she said, 'Please determine whose these are, the signet and cord, and staff.' So, Judah acknowledged them and said. She has been more righteous than I, because I did not give her to Shelah my son. And he never knew her again" (Genesis 38 and 2 -26). Both of her sons are listed in the genealogy of Jesus the Christ.

It says, "Abraham begot Isaac, Isaac begot Jacob, and Jacob begot Judah and his brother. Judah begot Perez and Zerah by Tamar" (Matthew 1 and 1-3). This passive is misleading in that it chronicles the lineage of Joseph, and not that Christ. Joseph bloodline had nothing to with the birth of Jesus.

The Gospels does not specify Mary's nationality. Instead, it slides her name in with the genealogy of her husband Joseph. As far as I suggest, Mary may have been a Canaanite, Egyptian, or Ethiopian woman. Afterall, all the patriarch's married, and bore the majority of their offspring with those women because their native wives were barren. The people of Krakow Poland sponsor tours to show off their Black Madonna of Czestochowa. They say, "The Black Madonna was painted by Saint Luke the Evangelist; and it was while painting the picture, Mary told him about the life of Jesus, which he later incorporated into his gospel. The next time we hear of the painting is in 326 A.D. when St Helen found it in Jerusalem and gave it to her son and had a shrine built for it in Constantinople (taken then brought to Rome). During a battle, the picture was placed on the walls of the city, and the enemy army fled. Our Lady saved the city from destruction. The picture was owned by many other people until 1382 when invading Tartars (Turks) attacked the fortress. A Tartar's arrow lodged into, and through the throat of the Madonna. The prince transferred the painting to a church in Czestochowa, Poland. When the Russians were at Warsaw's gates in 1920, thousands of people walked from Warsaw to Czestochowa to ask the Madonna for help. The poles defeated the Russians at a battle along the Wisla River. Pope John Paul II, a native son of Poland, prayed before the Madonna during his historic visit in 1979, several months after his election to the Chair of Peter (The Papacy). The Pope made another visit to Our Lady of Czestochowa in 1983, and again in 1991."

Saint Paul in his epistles implies that Jesus was cursed. It says, "Christ has redeemed us from the curse of the Law (Torah Laws) having become a curse for us. For it is written, Cursed is everyone who hangs on a tree, that the blessings of Abraham might come upon Gentiles in Christ Jesus, that we might receive the promise of the Spirit through faith" (Galatians 3 and 13). Why is not this allegation discussed in the religious community? I feel content saying that most Believers never marinated on this passage in their Holy Book.

However, the Holy Quran says this regarding Jesus and Satan. It says, "He (Baby Jesus) said; I am indeed a servant of Allah/God. He has given me the Book and made me a prophet: And He has made me blessed wherever I may be, and He has enjoined on me prayer and poor-rate insolent unblessed. And peace on me the day I was born, and the day I die, and the day I am raised to life. Such is Jesus' son of Mary statement of truth about which they dispute" (Sura 19 and 30-34, Mary).

And of Satan it says, "He said: O' Iblis (Satan), what prevented thee from submitting to him (Adam) whom I created with both My hands? Art thou proud or are thou of the exalted ones? He said: I am better than he; Thou hast created me of fire, and him Thou didst create of dust. He said: Go forth from hence! Surely, thou art driven away. And surely My curse is on thee to the day of Judgement." (Sura 38 and 75-78, Truthful God).

Here is a sermon, Saint John Chrysostom, a Fourth Century Christian Disciple, wrote, titled "Homilies Against The Jew." It says, "The Jews sacrifice their children to satan, they're worse than wild beasts, the synagogue is a brothel of den and scoundrels, a temple of demons devoted to adulterous cults a criminal assembly of Jews, a place of meetings for the assassins of Christ, a house of ill-fame. A dwelling of iniquities, a gulf, and abyss. The Jews have fallen into a condition lower than the vilest animal. Debauchery and drunkenness have brought them to the level of the lusty goat and pig. I hate the Jews because they violate the Law. I hate the synagogue because it has the Law and the Prophets. It is the duty of all Christians to hate the Jew." His homily was directed at the Ebionite or Nazarene Jews living in Palestine at that time. Imagine today, such inflammatory and pure hot hatred surfacing every year during the Celebration of the Risen? But the Attorney Reverend Bryant is free to exercise his free speech without impunity. So, he thought!

What I've uncovered, in plain view, is that the Lord God created in the book, only levy stiff, swift, and severe punishments against the nations it calls of Ham. While giving a wink to those of Shem and Japeth for the more hideous transgressions they sprout. The adhominous attacks against HAM was put in motion back in Genesis 17 and 4-5 when God added HAM to the covenant made with Abram. HAM was Gods final signature on His will, to be done on earth.

CHAPTER TEN
SIGNS OR SCIENCE, YOU DECIDE

The Tenak says, "God created man in His own image, in the image of God He created him, male and female" (Genesis 1 and 27). It then says, "The Lord God formed man of the dust of the ground, and breathed into his nostrils the breath of life, and man became a living being" (Genesis 2 and 7). Thereafter, it amends itself saying, "He took one of his (man) ribs and closed up the flesh in its place. Then the rib the Lord God had taken from man He made into a woman. And He brought her to the man" (Genesis 2 and 21-22). Is this passage Signs, or is it Science?

The Kebra Nagast says, "Then the Merciful One, the Lover of Mankind, answered them on behalf of Adam, and said unto them. You have I created out of fire and air (the Angels) with the one intent that ye should praise Me. Him have I created of twice as many elements as you; of dust and water, and of wind and fire, and he became a being of flesh and blood." Does this passage speak of Signs or Science?

The Holy Quran says, "We created you from dust, then from a small life-germ, then from a clot, then from a lump of flesh. We cause what We please to remain in the wombs (fetus) till an appointed time, then We bring you forth as babies, that you may attain your maturity. And of you is he who is caused to die" (Sura 22 and 1, The Pilgrimage). Does this Sura contain hidden Signs or is it Science? Or both?

The beginning of the book of Genesis implies that only two adults (Adam & Eve) existed on the earth. Then it introduces a serpent. Is this passage science or is it a sign of more than what meets the eyes? It says, "Now the serpent was more cunning than any beast of the field which the Lord God had made. And he said to the woman, Has God indeed said, You shall not eat of every tree of the garden" (Genesis 3 and 1). Right here it describes the serpent as He. In English, the proper noun describing Man or Male. Now we know there were more than two adults during the Genesis story. It then says, "Now Adam knew Eve (had relations), and she conceived and bore Cain. Then she bore again, this time his brother Abel" (Genesis 4 and 1-2). Now we have two other humankinds during the creation. Then it says this after Cain deletes his younger brother Abel. It says, "Then Cain went out from the presence of the Lord and dwelt in the land of Nod on the east of Eden. And Cain knew his wife, and she conceived" (Genesis 4 and 6-17).

Who and where did Cains wife come from if only three humanoids existed on the entire planet. The Book of Jubilee's (which was not selected to be part of the bible) says that her name was Awan who was his sister. But the daughters of Adam and Eve are not listed until after their third child was born. It say; "And Adam lived one hundred and thirty years, and begot a son in his own likeness, after his image (not God's image), and named him Seth. After he begot Seth, he had sons and daughter" (Genesis 5 and 3-4). So Awan was not Cain's sister, as legion suggests. She had to have been from a nation of people already in existence, living in the land of Nod east of the garden, where Cain was exiled.

As you peruse through the creation story you will find more and more humans appearing without details of how they arrived. Serpents cannot talk. So the serpent had to be human just like Eve for the two to communicate. I say a man because the pronoun He is used to describe it. John the Revelator says He is the Devil or Satan. It says, "He laid hold of the dragon, that serpent of old, who is the devil and satan (Revelations 20 and 2). Many legions suggest that Eve and the Serpent came into contact with each other numerous times. They discussed a particular tree and its fruits. Remember, that Eve and her husband had access to all the trees in the garden. It says, "Has God indeed said, You shall not eat of every tree of the garden, And the woman said to the serpent, We may eat the fruit of the trees of the garden, but of the fruit of the tree which is in the midst of the garden, God has said, You shall not eat it: (Genesis 3 and 1-3). The phrase "in the midst of the garden" is purely hullaballoo. It obscures our understanding. So this passage does not define the purpose of avoiding this tree. Could this tree be symbolic to a people, or a nation already in existence of the Genesis creation story? Let's dwell into that idea. There are many nations described as trees, and leaves in the book. It says, "Indeed Assyria was a cedar (a tree) in Lebanon, with fine branches that shaded the forest, And of high stature; And its top was among the thick boughs. The waters made it grow; Underground waters gave it height, with their rivers running around the place where it was planted And sent out little rivers to all the trees of the field, All the birds of the heavens made their nests in its boughs; Under its branches, all the beasts of the field brought forth their young; And in its shadow all great nations made their home. The cedars (Assyrians) in the garden of the fir trees were not like its boughs. And the chestnut trees were not like its branches; No tree in the garden of God was like it in beauty, I made it beautiful with a multitude of branches, So that all the trees of Eden envied it That were in the garden of God" (Ezekiel 31 and 3-9).

Is this passage describing plants, or a nation of people in existence living simultaneously with Adam and Eve? Namely the Assyrians. If cedar are people and nations in the book, then the trees in the garden that the book addresses are also peoples and nations.

Let's continue with the question about signs or science. The Kebra Nagast describes the Great Flood differently. It says, "To those who believed the word of their fathers and did His will, no injury came from the waters of the flood, but He delivered them, saying: If thou believest My work thou canst save thyself from the flood, And Noah said: O Lord, I believe Thy word, make me to know by what means I can be saved. And God said unto him: Thou canst be saved from the water by wood. Then Noah said: How, O Lord? And God said unto him: Make thyself a four-side ark and build it with the work of the carpenter, and make for it three stories inside, and go into it with all thy house. Noah believed the word of God, made the ark and was saved. God could have given unto Noah wings like the eagle and transported him to the country of the living with all his household, until His anger with sinners who had not believed the work of God had cooled; or He could have lifted him up into the air, or He could have commanded the water of the flood which was like a wall, not to approach the one mountain where He could make Noah to dwell with his sons, and not to submerge the beasts and cattle which he wanted. But know ye this, God was well pleased that by means of wood which had been sanctified, the salvation of His creation should take place...that is, through the ark and the wood of the Cross. God said unto Noah: Make that whereby thou shalt be saved, that is to say, the Tabernacle of the Church, and when He said unto him: Make it four-sided, He showed that the Sign of the Cross was fourfold. The four corners of the ark are the horns of the altar...and He commanded Moses to make the ark (Ark of the Covenant) out of indestructible wood. He said: I will sanctify thee from filth, from impurity, fornication, vindictiveness, and falsehood, together with thy brother and thy house. Now, sacrifice unto Me a clean sacrifice with cleanness, and I will accept thee after thou hast sanctified thyself and thy house; command all the people to sanctify themselves, for My holy things must be offered by holy ones." This passage describes The Flood as Gods way of purging the unbelievers and the Nephilim's, and not the entire world. It also implies that the that "the cross" is to be lifted.

Of the Nephilim's, it says, "The daughters of Cain with whom the angels had sinned conceived, but they were unable to bring forth their children and they died. Of the children which were in their wombs, some died and some did come forth by splitting open the bellies of their mother. They came forth by their navels, and when they were grown up they became giants whose height reached into the clouds; but for their sake and the sake of sinners, the wrath of God became quiet, and He said, My Spirit shall only rest on them for one hundred and twenty years then I will destroy them with the waters of the flood...them and all sinners who have not believed the Word of God." I ask the question, are these Signs or Science?

The Tenak says of Noah Ark, "And God said to Noah make yourself an ark of gopherwood. The length of the ark shall be three hundred cubits (450 feet long), its width fifty cubits (75 feet wide), and its height thirty cubits (45 feet high)" (Genesis 7 and 13-15). Then it says, "The waters prevailed fifteen cubits (22.2 feet high of water suffocated the earth) upward, and the mountains were covered. And all flesh died that moved on the earth and every man" (Genesis 7 and 20-21). The story said the water covered the earth for one hundred and fifty days, or five consecutive months. When the water receded, the living in the ark departed and repopulated the

128

earth. I was attached to an aircraft carrier in the U.S. Navy. The dimensions of that warship were one thousand ninety-two feet in length, one hundred thirty-four feet wide, with a flight deck the size of two football fields, it houses thousands of sailors, and weigh one hundred thousand tons. If you perform a simple vertical-torque-twist in a plain one-half mile into the heavens, that carrier immediately disappears. All you see beneath, is four or five sextillion tons of ocean and sea water. But Noah and his tiny Ark survived a planetarium calamity in a canoe boat. Is this passage science or is it signs?

The flood story put the first of humankind in Eastern Asia. The story says, "The waters receded continually from the earth. At the end of the hundred and fifty days the waters decreased. Then the ark rested in the mountains of Ararat" (Genesis 8 and 3-4). Mount Ararat is found in modern day Turkey. However, Iman's argue that the Ark rested in Mount Ararat in Saudi Arabia; the city of Mecca to be exact. This theory dispels the two hundred-thousand-year-old Homo sapient bones found near Ethiopia.

But if Noah and his family were the newest sapiens, then why would the radiometric testing of their bones and many other scriptural artifacts date back only ten thousand years? Is this story a sign or is it science?

The Injeel (gospels) says, "Then, behold, the veil of the temple was torn in two from top to bottom, and the earth quaked, and the rocks were split, the graves were opened; and many bodies of the saints who had fallen asleep were raised; and coming out of the graves after His (Christ) resurrection, they went into the holy city (Jerusalem) and appeared to many" (Matthew 27 and 51-53).

There are no other historians beside Saint Matthew, who spoke about this postmortem phenomenon. The Apostle said that the corpse appeared to many. So there should have been multiple accounts supporting this story. Beginning with the other Apostles who were there. How about from the living, the corpse encountered? How about from any of the centuries appointed by Pontius Pilate throughout the city of Jerusalem? You cannot find supporting support of this extraordinary claim in any of the Epistle's written to the church after the resurrection.

Staunch defenders of the Christian movement such as the African convert from Carthage, **Quintus Septimius Florens** Tertullian of 220 A.D., or the Greek Bishop Saint Irenaeus of the same time period, or Saint John Chrysostom of the fourth century did not describe this claim. After all, it is Saint Irenaeus who is accredited for choosing the four books to be used as the Gospels. Elaine Pagels, in her book "Beyond Belief" writes; Since Irenaeus saw the proof from prophecy as one way to resolve the problem of how to tell which prophecies and which revelations come from God, he added certain writings of the apostles to those of the prophets, since he, like Justin Martyr believed that together those constitute indispensable witness to truth. Like other Christians of their time Justin and Irenaeus, when they spoke of the Scriptures, had in mind primarily the Hebrew Bible; what we call the New Testament had not yet been assembled. Their conviction that God's truth is revealed in the events of salvation history provides the essential link between the Hebrew Bible and what Justin called the apostles memoirs which we know as the gospels of the New Testament. It was Irenaeus, so far as we can tell, who became the principal architect of what we call the four-gospel canon, the frame-work that includes in the New Testament collection the gospels, of Matthew, Mark, Luke, and John.

First Irenaeus denounces various Christian groups that settle on only one gospel, like the Ebionite Christian (who were Jews), who, he says, use only Matthew, or followers of Marcion, who use only Luke. Equally mistaken, Irenaeus continues, are those who invoke many gospels. Certain Christian, he says, declared that certain Christians boast that they have more gospels than there really are...but really, they have no gospel which is not full of blasphemy. Irenaeus resolved to hack down the forest of apocryphal and illegitimate writings like the Secret Book of James and the Gospel of Mary (or you can add those of the two prophetess Priest Maximilla and Priscilla who both said Jesus appeared to them in female form) and leave only four pillars standing. He boldly declared that the gospel, which contains all truth, can be supported by only these four pillars. Namely, the gospels attributed to Matthw, Mark, Luke, and John. To defend his choice, he declared that it is not possible that there can be either more or fewer than four, for just as there are four regions of the universe, and four principal winds, the church itself requires only four pillars. Furthermore, just as the prophet Ezekiel envisioned God's throne borne up by four living creatures, so the divine Word of God is supported by this four-form gospel. Following his lead; Christians in later generations took the faces of these four living creatures, the lion, the bull, the eagle, and the man as symbols of the four evangelists. What makes these gospels trustworthy, he claimed, is that their authors, who he believed included Jesus disciples Matthew and John, actually witnessed the events they related similarly, he added Mark and Luke, being followers of Peter and Paul, wrote down only what they had heard from the apostles themselves. Few New Testament scholars today would agree with Irenaeus we do not know who actually wrote these gospels, any more than we know who wrote the gospels of Thomas or Mary; all we know is that all of these gospels are attributed to disciples of Jesus. Nevertheless, Irenaeus not only welded the Gospel of John to the far more widely quoted gospels of

Matthew and Luke but praised John as the greatest gospel. For Irenaeus, John was not the fourth gospel, as Christians call it today, but the first and foremost of the gospels, because he believed that John alone understood who Jesus really is…God in human form. What God revealed in that extraordinary moment when he became flesh trumped any revelations received by mere human being, even prophets and apostles, let alone the rest of us. Henceforth all revelations endorsed by Christian leaders would have to agree with the gospels set forth in what would become the New Tew Testament. Through the centuries, these gospels have given rise to and extraordinary range of Christian art, music, poetry, theology, and legend. Yet Irenaeus recognized that even banishing all secret writings and creating a canon of four gospel accounts could not, by itself, safeguard the Christian movement. This is what happened in Irenaeus's congregation and, as we shall see, he responded by working to construct what he called orthodox (literally, straight-thinking) Christianity." Speaking of Priscilla do not dismiss her. She was known to have spent time with Saint Paul. He recognizes her when he wrote, "Greet Priscilla and Aquila, my fellow workers in Christ Jesus, who risked their own necks for my life to whom not only I give thanks, but also all the churches of the Gentiles. Likewise greet the church that is in their house. (Romans 16 and 3-5). I am not aware if the Prophetess Maximilla is mentioned in the New Testament, but she work alongside Priscilla. So Saint Paul should have known of her dedication as well.

I observe that the ancient scripts of that time period were more to do with Signs and warning for the people. For example, John the Revelator said, "I saw the heavens opened. He was clothed with a robe dipped in blood, and His name is called the Word of God. The armies in heaven, clothed in fine linen, white and clean followed Him on white horses (is this a description of the Changing of the

Guards at Buckingham Palace?). Out of his mouth goes a sharp sword, that with it He should strike the nations" (Revelations 19 and 11-15). The Revelator here is not speaking of him looking into a real heaven and viewing anything real thereafter. He says in the very beginning of his epistle that "I was in the Spirit on the Lord's Day" (Revelation 1 and 10). John saw nothing physical. Nor is he describing anything physical in his epistle. But is Saint John's revealing signs to come, or is it science?

John the Revelator identified what he saw in the heavens. He said, "And He who sat there was like a jasper and a sardine stone in appearance" (Revelations 4 and 3). Pull up a picture of a sardine stone, and there you will find what "He" appearance look like in human form. So the answer here is "written in the stone" (Earth, Wind, & Fire). Does this passage contain Science or Signs? You decide!

The Tenak gives us warnings of looking just for signs. It say, "If there arises among you a prophet or a dreamer of dreams, and gives you a sign or a Wonder, and the sign or Wonder comes to pass, of which he spoke of saying, Let us go after other god (meaning behaviors you may never have entertained; gambling, porn, lasciviousness), which you have not known, you shall not listen" (Deuteronomy 13 and 1-3).

It says, "I will give you shepherds (preachers) according to My heart, who shall feed you with knowledge and understanding" (Jeremiah 3 and 15). Then it says, "Both prophet and priest are godless, they commit adultery and live a lie. They strengthen the hands of evildoers, so that no one turns from wickedness" (Jeremiah 23 and 11-14).

When I hear simple minded, romper-room babbling in the mornings, of the first day of every calendar week, I get nauseated.

Here is one I heard on the radio in my car taking a drive. I think the lesson was Death & Dying:

"Why is everybody scared to die? All this week I had somebody come into my office and tell me they are afraid to die. You know what church? If the Lord call me Today... I'll go Tomorrow"!

Did you catch that last sentence?

This is the sort of rhetoric that morphs people into sheeple's (sheep peoples). Meaning they would follow in a surrender state of mine. Allowing their emotions to enter the realm, for the emotions to take control. For example, when Jesus was interrogated by one of the high priests; it says, "And when He had said these things, one of the officers who stood by struck Jesus with the palm of his hand, saying, do you answer the high priest like that?" (John 18 and 22). Spiritual emotionalism are the building blocks for all sorts of human terroristic behavior against other peoples, mostly against other sheeple's themselves. The most plausible reason why the Attorney Reverend Bryant submitted his article that was published in the Times Picayune was due to maliciousness and to publicly discredit a people disguised as religion. He spoke of "rhetoric" in his opening but did not address his malicious heart. Evil is a thought; the Devil is when that thought harms or injure others.

The Kebra Nagast says, "Satan hath no power whatsoever, for he hath only what he maketh to germinate in the mind. He cannot grasp firmly nor perform anything, he cannot beat, and he cannot drag away, he cannot seize, and he cannot fight; he can only make thoughts to develop silently in the mind. Then him who is caught by the evil mind, he prepares for destruction; but if a man hath conquered the evil mind he findeth grace and hath a reward which is everlasting."

In this book, I have open your consciousness to another sphere in which the average worshipper has not known. I have provided you with my sources, or precepts. It says, "For precept must be upon precept, line upon line, here a little, there a little" (Isaiah 27 and 10). I have provided you with the reference's I used from your holy books. My desire in this book is to command more critical dialogues and deeper discussions in your meetings. I also wish that this book be used and discussed in the schools of Seminary-Training so that people who have genuine aspirations; in their search for solace, to fill that empty void we all have, including animals, find in themselves the RUACH HA' QODESH or, the true Holy Spirit in themselves, and not the evil one. I cannot express the record of myself on paper, let alone a deity. No one has that ability. The Holy Quran says, "If all the trees in the earth were pens, and the sea with seven more seas added to it were ink, the words of Allah/God would not be exhausted" (Sura 31 and 27 Luqman, The Ethiopian).

To offer an opposing view of the whole theology spectrum, Christopher Hitchens shared his opinion and his interpretation of the subject. He wrote in his book, "There are some very obvious objections to be made to this. In the first place, several such disclosures have been claimed to occur, at different times and places, to hugely discrepant prophets or mediums. In some cases, most notably the Christian, one revelation is apparitions, with the promise of a further but ultimate one to come. In other cases, the opposite difficulty occurs, and the divine instruction is delivered, only once, and for the final time, to an obscure personage whose lightest word then becomes law. Since all of these revelations, many of them hopelessly inconsistent, cannot by definition be simultaneously true, it must follow that some of them are false and illusory. It could also follow that only one of them is authentic, but in the first place this seems dubious and in the second place, it appears to necessitate religious war in order to decide whose revelation is the true one. A further difficulty is the apparent tendency of the Almighty to reveal himself only to unlettered and quasi-historical individuals, in regions of Middle Eastern wasteland that were long the home of idol worship and superstition, and in many instances already littered with existing prophecies. The syncretic tendencies of monotheism, and the common ancestry of the tales, mean in effect, that a rebuttal to one is a rebuttal to all. Horribly and hatefully though they may have fought with one another, the three monotheisms, claim to share a descent at least from the Pentateuch of Moses, and the Koran certifies Jes as People of the book, Jesus as a prophet, and a virgin as his mother.

Interestingly the Koran does not blame the Jews for the murder of Jesus (he is correct, the Quran says, "And for their saying: We have killed the Messiah Jesus, son of Mary the messenger of Allah, and they killed him not, nor did they cause his death on the cross, but he was made to appear to them as such. And certainly, those who differ therein are in doubt about it. They have no knowledge about it, but only follow a conjecture, and they killed him not for certain" Sura 4 and 157, The Women). It also accepts Judaism as God's chosen one. It says, "Allah speaks the truth; so follow the religion of Abraham, the upright one. And he was not one of the polytheists" Sura 3 and 94 The Family of Amran), but it also says, And the Jews say, The Christians follow nothing good, and the Christians say, The Jews follow nothing good, while they recite the same Book. So Allah will judge between them on the day of Resurrection in that wherein they differ" Sura 2 and 113, The Cow); as one book of the Christian new Testament does, but this is only because it makes the bizarre claim that someone else was crucified by the Jews in his place. The foundation story of all three faiths concerns the purported meeting between Moses and god, at the summit of Mount Sinai. This in turn led to the handing down of the Decalogue, or Ten Commandments. The tale is told in the second book of Moses, known as the book of Exodus, in chapters 20-40. Most attention has been concentrated on chapter 20 itself, where the actual commandments are given. It should not perhaps be necessary to summarize and expose these, but the effort is actually worthwhile." He then writes, "It would be harder to find an easier proof that religion is manmade. There is, first the monarchical growling about respect and fear, accompanied by a stern reminder of omnipotence and limitless revenge, of the sort with which a Babylonian or Assyrian emperor might have ordered the scribes to begin a proclamation. There is then a sharp reminder to keep working and only to relax when the absolutist says so. Then there is the very salient question of what the commandments do not say. Is it too modern to notice that there is nothing about the protection of children from cruelty, nothing about slavery, and nothing about genocide? Or is it too exactingly in context to notice that some of these very offenses are about to be positively recommended"?

Well, the Christians had been at work on the same wishful attempt at proof long before the Zionist school of archaeology began to turn a spade. Saint Paul's Epistle to the Galatians had transmitted god's promise to the Jewish patriarchs, as an unbroken patrimony, to the Christians, and in the nineteenth and early twentieth centuries, you could hardly throw away an orange peel in the Holy Land without hitting a fervent excavator. General Gordon, the biblical fanatic later slain by the Mahdi at Khartoum, was very much to the fore. William Albright of Baltimore was continually vindicating Joshua's Jericho and other myths. Some of these diggers, even given the primitive techniques of the period, counted as serious rath than merely opportunistic.

Morally serious too: the French Dominican archaeologist Roland de Vaux gave a hostage to fortune by saying that 'if the historical faith of Israel is not founded in history, such faith is erroneous, and therefore, our faith is also.' A most admirable and honest point, on which the good father may now be taken up."

He concludes, "One could go through the Old Testament book by book, here pausing to notice a lapidary phrase 'Man is born to trouble,' as the book of Job says, and there a fine verse, but always encountering the same difficulties. People attain impossible ages and yet conceive children. Mediocre individuals engage in single combat or on-on-one argument with god or his emissaries, raising afresh the whole question of divine omnipotence or even divine commonsense, and the ground is forever soaked with the blood of the innocent. Moreover, the context is oppressively confined and local. None of these provincials, or their deity, seems to have any idea of a world beyond the desert, the flocks and herds, and the imperatives of nomadic subsistence. This is forgivable on the part of the provincial yokels, obviously, but then what of their supreme guide and wrathful tyrant? Perhaps he was made in their image, even if not graven?

I conclude with this passage from the Gospel of Thomas, in Professor Pagels books:

Jesus said, "The kingdom is inside you, and outside you. When you come to know yourselves, then you will be known, and you will see that it is you who are the children of the living Father."

Thank you for your most expensive gift, that is your time!

BIBLIOGRAPHIES

Ali, Maulana, Muhammad, "The Antichrist and Gog and Magog," Ah madiyya anjuman Isha at Islam, Lahore Inc, Columbus Ohio, 1992, page 10).

Ali, Maulana, M., "The Holy Qur'an Arabic Test, English Translation," by Ahmadiyah Anjuman Isha'at Islam, LaHore, Inc, 1995.

Brooks, Miguel, F., "Kebra Nagast, The Glory of the Kings," The Red Sea Press, Inc., Lawrence, New Jersey, 2002, pages 124-125, 146-149.

Churchill, Ward, and Wall, Jim V., "The COINTELPRO Papers," South End Press, Boston, MA.

Dershowitz, Alan, M., "The Genesis of Justice," published by Time Warner Company, copyright 2000, Pages 99-100, 246-258.

Didier, Carlos "Jesuit Extreme Oath of Induction," by Subterranean Rome, published in 1843, New York, NY.

Feldman, Ari, "Why Did 23andMe Tell Ashkenazi Jews They Could Be Descended from Khazars?," The Forward, August 2017.

Ford, Henry, "The International Jew," published by ReadaClassic.com, copyright 2011, page 24-25, 108, and 141.

Ginzberg, Louis, Jastrow, Morris, Jr., Kohler, Kaufmann, Levi, Gerson B., "Bithiah," Jewish Encyclopedia, 1901-1906.

Hagins, Ray, "The Verdict Is In" video, The African Village, Saint Louis, Missouri, 2005.

Hitchens, Christopher, "god Is Not Great," Twelve Hatchet Book Group, New York, NY, 2007, pages 97-107, 205-206.

Jain, Richa., "The History Behind SATI, A Banned Funeral Practice in India, Cultural Trips, May 2018.

Levy, Sholomo., "General Description of the Black Jewish or Hebrew Israelite Community," Beth Elohim Hebrew Congregation, Saint Albans, NY.

Pagels, Elaine, "Beyond Belief, The Secret Gospels of Thomas," The Random House Publishing Group, New York, pages 6, 11, 31-32, 54 and 64, 110-115.

Rapoport, Louis, "The Lost Jews," Stein and Day publisher, New York, pages 62-65, and 161-172.

ABOUT THE AUTHOR

Mr. Rowan is a Foundation Black American, meaning his parents did not immigrate to his country. His lineage can be traced back to the first segregated Census taken in 1860 and beyond. He was born in the Big-Easy, where both his parents emigrated too, from neighboring Mississippi. Mr. Rowan is a graduate of Loyola University, in New Orleans, Louisiana, he completed the Federal Law Enforcement Training Center (FLET-C) in Glynco, Georgia, he is a veteran of the United States Navy, where he was attached to the carrier USS AMERICA (CV-66) and was awarded Three Ribbons and Two Medals during his brief tour. He retired from twenty-five years of public service, and is the owner of a small LLC in his resident State of Northwest Florida. You may follow him on his website at TeamBFM.net where you can purchase his book, and other merchandise, as well as read his blogs, and leave positive comments. Please click on the donate button and follow the instructions there if you enjoy his contents.

Printed in the USA
CPSIA information can be obtained
at www.ICGtesting.com
LVHW020833071024
792988LV00017B/823

9 781088 122747